£7.95

D1572184

PENNINE ALPS WEST

MT. COLLON N face

Pennine Alps West

GRANDES DENTS - BOUQUETINS - COLLON
PIGNE - AIGS. ROUGES - CHEILON - RUINETTE
OTEMMA - VALPELLINE NORTH - GRAND COMBIN

companion volumes
Pennine Alps East
Pennine Alps Central

compiled and edited by
ROBIN G. COLLOMB

Alpine Club   London

PENNINE ALPS WEST

First published in Britain 1979 by

The Alpine Club   London

Copyright © 1979 by West Col Productions

SBN 900523 30 1

Produced from computer information storage and retrieval systems
developed from volumes published under the title
Selected Climbs in the Pennine Alps (Neill) 1962 (one vol.)
Selected Climbs in the Pennine Alps (Collomb) 1968 (two vols.)

Revised and re-written in three vols. as –
Pennine Alps East (1975)
Pennine Alps Central (1975)
Pennine Alps West (1979)

Code: PAW.   Serial 83B, March, 1979

Photography and diagrams:
Frischer-Roberts Archives 1961-1979
West Col Archives 1946-1979
Photographic processing: Ray Hebron

Designed, produced and sold for the Alpine Club by
West Col Productions
Goring   Reading   Berks. RG8 9AA

Printed offset in England by Swindon Press Ltd, Swindon, Wilts.

Contents

Introduction   11

    Preface to 1979 edition - Maps - Altitudes and
    nomenclature - Orientation - Camping - Grading
    of climbs

Valley Bases   16
- Arolla valley   16
- Dix barrage (Val d'Hérémence)   17
- Val de Nendaz   17
- Mauvoisin (Val de Bagnes)   17
- Val d'Entremont (Gd. St. Bernard)   18
- Valpelline   19
Valle di Ollomont (By cwm)   19

SECTION ONE   21
Arolla and Dix basins
    Mountain bases   22
    Grandes Dents chain   36
    Bouquetins-Brulé chain   61
    Collon-Pigne-Aigs. Rouges groups   75
    Cheilon-Pleureur-Rosablanche chain   110

SECTION TWO   139
Frontier chain
    Mountain bases   140
    Otemma-Valpelline North chain   145
    Morion chain   176

SECTION THREE   183
Combin area
    Mountain bases   184
    Grand Combin group   189

By-Valsorey-Velan frontier ridge   211

Addenda for East and Central area guides   222
Index of routes shown on diagrams   225
General Index   229

Diagrams

Mt. Collon N face	frontis.
Comba d'Oren - Valpelline	35
Veisivi WSW (Arolla) side	37
Gde. Veisivi NW ridge	40
Blanche de Perroc NW face	42
Grandes Dents from SW	47
Aig. de la Tsa from NE	55
Douves Blanches SW ridge	58
Bouquetins E side	64
Bouquetins W side	67
Col Collon SW side	70
Mt. Brulé N side	73
Mt. Collon - l'Evêque W side	78
Mt. Collon - l'Evêque E side	83
Mt. Collon N face	88
Petit Mt. Collon N face	93
Pigne d'Arolla SE side	96
Pigne d'Arolla N side	96
Aigs. Rouges d'Arolla from ENE	104
Aigs. Rouges d'Arolla E face	107
Mt. Blanc de Cheilon from SW	111
Mt. Blanc de Cheilon N face	117
La Ruinette SW side	122
La Ruinette NW face	126
Pte. d'Otemma W side	126
Luette-Pleureur NE side	129
La Rosablanche, map	134
Mt. Fort W flank	134
Mt. Fort hut looking SE	138

Otemma frontier ridge	141
Valpelline North frontier ridge, SE side	152
La Singla E side	156
La Singla W side	157
Col Collon hut looking SW	159
Aouille Tseuque N ridge	163
Bec d'Epicoune N ridge	167
Mt. Gelé NE side	167
Grand Combin N side	195
Mt. Durand glacier	198
Grand Combin SW side	201
Grand Combin from WNW	204
Combin de Corbassière, Petit Combin from NE	209
Mt. Velan W side	215
Mt. Velan from NE	219

INTERNATIONAL ALPINE DISTRESS SIGNAL

A more elaborate system of signals has been
devised in Britain but the International system
is basic to the subject of attracting attention
in an emergency.

Use a whistle, torch or flashes of the sun on
a mirror. Alternatively, shout, or wave
bright clothing:

Six regular flashes/notes in a minute, repeated
at intervals of a minute.

The reply is three signals per minute.

ABBREVIATIONS

AC	Alpine Club
Aig.	Aiguille
biv.	bivouac (hut)
c.	approximately
CAAI	Italian Universities Alpine Club
CAI	Italian Alpine Club
Dt(s).	Dent(s)
gl.	glacier
Gd(s)	Grand(e)s
h.	hour(s)
IGM	Italian military map
Ital.	Italian
km.	kilometre(s)
L	left (direction)
LK	Swiss federal map
m.	metre(s)
min.	minute(s)
mtn.	mountain
pt.	point (spot height)
Pta.	Punta
Pte.	Pointe (summit)
R	right (direction)
Rpt.	report from correspondent
rte(s).	route(s)
SAC	Swiss Alpine Club

Compass directions are indicated as: N, S, E, W, NE, SW, etc.

Introduction

The previous guidebook to the Pennine Alps (Alpine Club, 1968) attempted to deal with the entire range in two volumes. This proved possible because large areas of ground at the eastern and western ends of the range were omitted or only covered by brief notes. In general throughout the entire length of the range, the Italian side received perfunctory treatment. This was partly due to economics in the amount of information that could be published, lack of first hand accounts and general ignorance of the Italian valleys. A lot of this can now be corrected but once again economics are the ruling force and only the most important information in mountaineering terms can be included where previously nothing had been published.

The result is a guidebook for the Pennine Alps in three volumes, of which the second and third are much larger than the first. Moreover, the Western volume has been published four years after the Eastern and Central volumes, resulting in a tendency towards imbalance with the first two, both in content and attitude towards the western area as a whole. Had the western guide been published earlier it would have undoubtedly contained more information. British parties still visit this region infrequently and mostly go to Arolla or the Chanrion hut, occasionally to the Swiss Valsorey area. This leaves the editor and his assistants still wondering why the material has been expanded nearly 100% over the content of the 1968 guide. The divisions of the range are now as follows:

I PENNINE ALPS EAST
Simplonpass to Monte Moropass and the Neues Weisstor
Weissmies, Portjengrat, Mischabel chains.

II PENNINE ALPS CENTRAL
Neues Weisstor to Col des Bouquetins
Monte Rosa, Matterhorn, Dent Blanche, Weisshorn
chains, Italian valley ranges, Valpelline South.

III PENNINE ALPS WEST
Col des Bouquetins to Gd. St. Bernard pass
Grandes Dents chain, Bouquetins, Collon-Pigne-Aigs. Rouges,
Valpelline North-Otemma chain, Grand Combin, Mt. Velan.

In contrast with hundreds of letters and route descriptions received from correspondents for Pennine Alps East and Central,
less than 50 have come in for Pennine Alps West in a period
now exceeding ten years. Only three journey descriptions have
been received in this period, from Sir Anthony Rawlinson, Eric
Roberts and Jeremy Talbot. Roberts, as usual, has contributed
a considerable amount of additional information, as one might
expect from the most widely travelled Alpine climber among
living Englishmen today.

The introductory matter of Pennine Alps East and Central
contains a description of technical source publications consulted, and a selected English bibliography, which are excluded
from this volume.

An exhaustive edition of this guide to the Pennine Alps will
probably never be published in English. But we may reasonably
suppose in the course of time to see a further improved edition
with more complete coverage of the many sub-ranges and
divisions of this magnificent part of the Alps.

Robin G. Collomb
Goring Heath, March 1979

MAPS

The guide is designed for use with the new Swiss federal grid map (LK) drawn in a scale of 1/25,000. Equally good is the LK 1/50,000 map which comes in a grid series and tourist series, but naturally it has features only half the size and reduced detail. The Swiss map extends right across the crest zone of the range into Italy so that in general the official Italian map (IGM) has not been consulted. The following maps refer to the entire Pennine Alps range (all available from West Col Productions):

1:25,000 grid series

1287 Sierre	1325 Sembrancher	1347 Matterhorn
1288 Raron	1326 Rosablanche	1348 Zermatt
1289 Brig	1327 Evolène	1349 Monte Moro
1306 Sion	1328 Randa	1365 Gd. St. Bernard
1307 Vissoie	1329 Saas	1366 M. Velan
1308 St. Niklaus	1345 Orsières	
1309 Simplon	1346 Chanrion	

1:50,000 grid series

273 Montana	283 Arolla	292 Courmayeur
274 Visp	284 Mischabel	293 Valpelline
282 Martigny	285 Domodossola	294 Gressoney

1:50,000 district series

5003 Mont Blanc-Grand Combin   5006 Zermatt und Umgebung

1:100,000 grid series

41 Col du Pillon	46 Val de Bagnes
42 Oberwallis	47 Monte Rosa

In view of the large number of maps involved, sheet numbers in the 1/25,000 scale series are given for all major entries in the guidebook.

ALTITUDES AND NOMENCLATURE

All heights are taken from LK 25, either from fixed points or contour calculations extracted from this map. Place names come from the same map, and where appropriate commonly used Italian alternative names are given as well.

ORIENTATION

The directions left (L) and right (R) in the sense of direction of movement of the climber - ascent, descent, traverse of slope - have been used consistently throughout. For mtn. features such as glaciers, couloirs, rivers, etc. the traditional orographical reference to left and right banks as viewed in the direction of flow, i.e. downward, has been abandoned, due to the number of complaints received over the confusion this system causes. These features are therefore now described in the sense of movement of the climber. For example, you go up the L side of a glacier, which was previously described as ascending the R bank. In some descriptions both ways are given to emphasise orientation. Compass directions are also given to assist with route finding.

CAMPING

Most valley bases (see next section) have authorised campsites, and the impecunious seeking cheaper camping can usually find other permissible sites with no facilities for nominal charges.

GRADING OF CLIMBS

In accordance with the UIAA classification system, the grading of rock climbs is numerical from I to VI and A1 to A4 for artificial. Grade I is the easiest and VI the hardest. Variations in difficulty are denoted by + and - signs; plus is above the normal rating and minus below (i.e. V-/V/V+). These

14

variations above grade IV will matter for the expert climber and should be equally helpful in the lower grades for the average performer. It must be stressed that the grade of a climb is determined not only by pure technical difficulty but also by objective danger and length.

Mixed climbs and snow/ice routes are also graded in six stages. This grading is always more approximate and less precise than the numerical rock grades because of variable conditions in a season and from year to year. Winter climbing will be different again, and apart from severe cold grades could be lower or higher according to the nature of the route. In order of rising difficulty: F (easy), PD (moderately difficult), AD (fairly difficult), D (difficult), TD (very difficult), ED (extremely difficult). Further refinement is possible by adding plus or minus signs.

Valley bases

AROLLA VALLEY

   This valley is the western fork of the Val d'Hérens. Post bus service Sion-Les Haudères-Arolla (41 km.) several times a day in summer. Arolla (1998m.) is the most important climbing centre in the Western Pennines and overlaps to some extent with the Zermatt district. All classes of hotels and pensions, several shops, good food provisioning, main public services, guides' bureau, tourist office. Private cars can be taken to the village centre which is imperfectly shown on all maps at present. A new motor road zigzags W above the valley to the village square. The Pralong family which manages the post office and runs a sports shop, chalet rental and dormitory accommodation is very pro-British and will always give advice and assistance to newcomers.

   Camping is something of a hardship at Arolla. From the late 1940s to the early 1970s this has been carried out mostly along the E bank of the Borgne anywhere above La Monta hamlet for a distance of one km., up to below Arolla itself. No facilities and generally numerous small sloping sites for tents, about 20 min. walking distance from village centre. Camping here is now being discouraged. Hotels in the valley have been offering camping for a limited number of tents with facilities provided. Fields adjoining the village may now be used with permission. Inquire at the post office for current situation and procedure for camping. Visitors with their own cars will find it more convenient to camp at a good authorised site at Evolène.

The village road continues in zigzags through forest to the W, called Fontanesses, an area of new residences and hotels, not shown on map. The main valley road continues for $2\frac{1}{2}$ km. to the moraines of the Lower Arolla gl., ample carparking.

DIX BARRAGE (Val d'Hérémence)

Not really a valley base although there are modest inns at Pralong (1608m.) and Le Chargeur (2102m.), the latter being the post bus terminus, 28 km. from Sion. Buses several times a day to below the great dam wall of the Dix artificial lake, itself a big tourist attraction. A cableway goes to the top of the dam wall and there is a motor boat service down the lake, so that the Dix hut can be reached by almost everyone. This explains the high frequency for this hut, as a smaller number undertake the much longer walk from Arolla. Food shop and restaurants at Le Chargeur.

VAL DE NENDAZ

Bus service Sion-Haute Nendaz-Super Nendaz (1733m.). Two inns, limited facilities. The road forks, one branch going to Tortin (2039m.), a hamlet near the E part of the Mt. Gelé cableway system; some buses go to this point, 19 km. from Sion. The other branch (no buses) goes up to the barrage pumping station on top of the Cleuson lake (2186m.), then along the NE side of the lake to the Tsamos pasture (2259m.). Carparking. Above this point a jeep road twists to the St. Laurent hut. See Rte. 14. No formal campsites anywhere in the upper valley.

MAUVOISIN (Val de Bagnes)

Bus service from Martigny via Sembrancher-Le Châble (railway to this point)-Champsec-Lourtier-Fionnay-Mauvoisin. Above Le Châble are the Verbier village resorts (bus service)

17

and the main W branches of the Mt. Gelé cableway system which can be used to approach the Mt. Fort hut. Higher up the Val de Bagnes, Fionnay village (1489m.), 29 km. from Martigny, is an attractive mtn. resort with good facilities and a small camp ground. The bus terminus at Mauvoisin (1841m.), 36 km. from Martigny, has only inn accommodation in summer (closed in winter). The road up to the barrage and along the W shore of the lake is rough but motorable for cars (stonefall hazard) to the Lancet bridge (2040m.), but drivers are advised to park before this point. Beyond the Lancet bridge the road is only suitable for jeeps. See Rte. 16.

VAL D'ENTREMONT (Gd. St. Bernard road)

Bus service Martigny-Sembrancher-Orsières (railway to this point), Liddes, Bourg St. Pierre, Bourg St. Bernard, Gd. St. Bernard pass.

A much frequented valley in summer, crowded with motor traffic plying between Switzerland and Italy. Mountain visitors will not be interested in any point below Bourg St. Pierre (1632m.), now something of a backwater and bypassed by the new main road. It remains a pleasant and quiet centre, with shops, hotels, inns and all the usual facilities, campsites, 32 km. from Martigny. The new road is now largely covered by an avalanche roof along to Bourg St. Bernard, also called Super St. Bernard (1915m.), at the entrance to the tunnel. Small general provision shop, inns and hotels, limited services in summer because this is primarily a winter skiing area. Camping possible with hoteliers' permission. The tunnel (toll charge) underpasses the road over the col. The original road continues for summer traffic over the top. At the Gd. St. Bernard pass (2469m.), no attractions for the climber but a veritable bazaar more like an oriental market place for souvenir-hunting tourists. Frequent traffic-jams. The ascent/descent on the Italian side of the pass is shorter and more

18

continuously steep, with Aosta town at the bottom. Good bus service from Aosta to top of pass.

ITALIAN

VALPELLINE

One of the longest and most remote valleys in the Pennine Alps. Bus service from Aosta town up the Gd. St. Bernard road and into the valley to reach Valpelline village (960m.), all main services. This infrequent service continues to Oyace (1390m., inns and shop). Just before Dzovenno (1575m.), with a couple of inns, is a campsite on the Essert meadow, on S side of road, with carpark and access across a field towards three little tarns in the forest nearby. Seek permission from inn beside carpark. The road reaches Bionaz (1606m., small inn, difficult to buy provisions), the bus terminus, 25 km. from Aosta. No public transport above this point, the good road continues past hamlets up to the Place Moulin barrage, large carpark beside dam wall (c. 1950m.), 32 km. from Aosta. No facilities of any description. A short distance below carpark is a slip road leading down to the Place Moulin inn (c. 1900m.), simple accommodation and meals. Camping possible beside inn with the innkeeper's permission; space for two tents. The rough jeep road rising across N side of lake, and above the new footpath leading to Prarayer, is forbidden to motorists. Detail shown on all maps at present is partly incorrect.

VALLE DI OLLOMONT (By cwm)

An important branch of the Valpelline, road junction just beyond Valpelline village (see above). From here a good road goes up to Ollomont (1356m.), inns, shops, bus terminus, 17 km. from Aosta. The road continues, fairly narrow, through

Vaud hamlet to ample carparking at the Glacier roadhead (1549m.) in another 3 km. Stall for snacks in summer, no other facilities. This spot is enclosed by a headwall under the huge By cwm.

AROLLA & DIX BASINS

Mountain bases

Tsa Hut   2607m.

LK 1347.   Cabane de la Tsa. Property of the Val d'Hérens guides, open to all. Constructed in 1975. Not marked on map, situated on the small shoulder pt. 2607m. directly above (E of) La Monta hamlet just below Arolla, and below the Pte. de Tsalion.   Warden in summer, simple restaurant service, 60 places.

1 Only the lower part of approach track is shown on map. From Arolla post office descend the first road zigzag to the section which continues up the valley. A few m. in the opposite direction a path leaves the road and crosses the main river by a good bridge.   On the other side continue by a small very steep twisting track almost due E in wooded slopes. It eventually bears L (NE) at an easier angle and crosses the Roussette stream.   Continue diagonally NE up big grass and stone slopes called La Tsa towards an obvious shoulder in the broad ridge ahead. Reach this from the R then bear L on to the promontory where the hut is situated (2-2½ h.).

Bertol Hut   3311m.

LK 1347.   Cabane de Bertol. SAC, new in 1976 near site of previous building, on a narrow rock buttress immediately N of the Col de Bertol. Warden, restaurant service, 80 places.

2 From Arolla the contractors' road up the valley can be walked or driven to the service cableway at pt. 2092m. on the frontal moraine of the Bas Arolla gl. (45 min. on foot). Car-parking.   Take a path NNE to join the original footpath at pt. 2201m. Return R and follow path across rockbands to cross the Bertol stream at pt. 2336m. After several zigzags the path divides at the end of terraced workings (signpost). Climb steeply L (NE) over rough ground in many zigzags to the upper Plan de Bertol (hut, 2664m.) (1¼ h.). The path continues at an easier angle over grass, stones and moraine NE to the Bertol gl., which is mounted towards a rognon in the centre. Turn this barrier on the R and go up a snow cwm E. Trend L, cross a bergschrund and climb rocks in the last snow slope (paint flashes) to reach the <u>Col de Bertol</u> (3269m.) by a fairly steep snow slope. Go up to the foot of a large broken buttress on the N side and climb this by cut steps and cables, (2 h., 4 h. from Arolla).

Note: From Zermatt (Pennine Alps Central area), by Schönbiel hut (4 h.) and over the Col d'Hérens to Bertol hut (6½ h., 10½ h. from Zermatt without halts).

Bertol - Aosta huts connection, see Rte. 18.

<u>Bouquetins Bivouac</u>   2980m.

LK 1327. Bivouac des Bouquetins. SAC, new in 1975, not marked on map. Situated on moraine forming a broad hump and prominent corner where the Haut Arolla gl. bends in descent from NW to N, on its true R bank. The moraine hump lies immediately below and S of pt. 3086.5m. Door open, utensils and water carriers, stove for cooking but simpler to take your own stove, places and blankets for 15.

3   From Arolla follow Rte. 2 to the end of the terraced workings where the Bertol rte. climbs back NE. Continue straight ahead (S) along a path going down a little before turning L (E) and rising across the lower Plan de Bertol, just N of pt. 2615.6m., to traverse E under a rockband and reach the large lateral moraine on the L (E) side of the Haut Arolla gl. at c. 2540m. None of this section is shown as a path on LK25, but is marked on LK50. A small track follows the moraine till it peters out in ice towards the middle of the gl. Continue straight up on ice and rubble due S, keeping some distance from the L (E) bank, until opposite the moraine corner where the biv. is situated. Approach this in a wide circle to the L, to avoid small groups of crevasses, and return N to mount the moraine bank (track) near biv. (3 h. from Arolla).

Vignettes - Bouquetins huts connection (across the Col de l'Evêque)

4 This col is frequented for making several important expeditions, including the High Level Route, and frequency will increase because of the convenience this hut connection affords in enabling climbs not previously accessible from the Vignettes hut to be made without descending to Arolla. A fine gl. crossing, crevasses need caution, splendid scenery. F/F+.

From the Vignettes hut follow a path in the rock ridge W to the Col des Vignettes. Now cross a snow terrace horizontally S and pass R (W) of pt. 3162m. to drop down a short steep slope on to the Col de Chermotane (3053m.). Work SE over the plateau of the Mt. Collon gl., trending R after passing under the N face of the Petit Mt. Collon, and finally climbing always at an easy angle S towards the Ptes. d'Oren on the frontier ridge ahead. More numerous crevasses, with the Col du Petit Mt. Collon on your R. Trend L without incident and reach the broad saddle of the Col de l'Evêque (3392m.) (2¼ h.).

On the other side go down a snowfield almost due E to the edge of a steeper crevassed zone. Keep R and join the stony frontier ridge on the R near pt. 3263.7m. Follow this ridge down to Col Collon (3087m.) (30 min.). Now descend on snow due N for 15 min. before bearing R (E) under the large rock island of La Vierge to reach in another 15 min. to the NE the moraine corner where the hut is perched (1¼ h. from Col de l'Evêque, 3½ h. from Vignettes hut. In reverse direction, same time).

Col Collon - Bouquetins huts connection (across Col Collon)

5 This connection is more likely to be used by parties coming out of the Valpelline into the Arolla basin, and is therefore described in this S-N direction. An easy crossing, short, F. By combining the previous rte., the connection between the Col Collon and Vignettes huts across the Col de l'Evêque will be obvious.

From the Col Collon hut take a small traverse track NE over rocky ground, often snow covered, and reach moraines at pt. 2833m. where the main track, cairns, from the valley bed below is joined. Follow traces of a track and cairns in a rising curve to the R (E), up a central moraine in large snowbeds. When below the col to the N, bear L up rubble to pt. 3098m. above short rock barriers. A short horizontal section on snow leads N to the col (3087m.) (1 h.). Now follow the previous rte. to the Bouquetins biv. (about $1\frac{3}{4}$ h. from Col Collon hut; to Vignettes hut, $3\frac{3}{4}$ h.).

Note: Bouquetins - Aosta huts connection, see Rte. 19.

Vignettes Hut

LK 1347. Cabane des Vignettes. SAC, situated on a rock spine running E from the Col des Vignettes and E of the Pigne d'Arolla, directly opposite the Bertol hut on the other side of the Arolla valley. One of the most frequented huts in the Western Pennines. Warden and restaurant service, 128 places.

6 From Arolla follow the main road up the valley, over a bridge (1973m.) to a signposted path on the R in 3 min. from bridge. Go up wooded then grassy slopes and old moraine past a junction at pt. 2204m. (path coming in from N from upper Arolla village and new access road) to the moraine crest curving W to S, which marks the R side of the Pièce gl. Follow the moraine to a sluice gate in the torrent below the gl. Take a signposted path L (old way and winter rte. to R) and follow cairns S, keeping close to the base of the gl. on your R. The

path zigzags over smooth glaciated rocks and finally reaches
the gl. near pt. 2760m. under the Vuibé rocks. Ascend the
gl. on this side with a steep section under pt. 3051.5m. to the
upper plateau, then bear R (SW) over snow slopes to the Col
des Vignettes. Turn L (E) along a rock spine to reach the hut
which is situated on the R (S) side (3½ h., 1¾ h. in descent).

Chanrion - Vignettes huts connection

7 Up the Otemma gl. and over the broad Col de Chermotane
(3053m.). A trade rte. From the Chanrion hut there are
upper and lower approaches to the Otemma gl. Upper: A
vague track mounts E over grass and scree to a small but well
defined traverse path. This works SE below a large rockband
and over steep grass then scree to reach a promontory (2720m.)
overlooking the gl. From here descend an easy scree couloir
facing SE for some distance, then traverse L on to the gl. at
c. 2600m. (1¼ h.). Lower: Follow a descending path S to jeep
road at pt. 2414m. and take this to a bend above chalets at
pt. 2337m. Short-cut this loop. Either join the original path
in a few min. which rises a little round shoulder 2467m. before
descending then traversing to finish on top of a rockface at
lower end of the Otemma gl. Or take jeep road at a lower
level, via pt. 2329m. which ends at the base of the rockface,
pt. 2357m. Either way, traverse on to the gl., somewhat loose
and unpleasant, work into the middle and go up without incident
to the low, broad and distinct snow saddle of the col (3 h.,
4¼ h. from hut).

From the col bear L and cross almost level snow N to a
short steep slope rising to a shoulder immediately L of
pt. 3162m. Continue horizontally in the same direction across
a snow terrace to the Col des Vignettes, then turn R along a
track in a rock spine to the Vignettes hut (45 min., 5 h. from
Chanrion hut, about same time in reverse direction which is
especially tiring in the afternoon heat).

<u>Aiguilles Rouges (Waldkirch) Hut</u>   2810m.

LK 1326, 1327, 1347. Cabane des Aiguilles Rouges. Property of the Geneva University Alpine Club, open to all. Situated on a scree and rock rib at the outer edge of the Aigs. Rouges gl. cwm, almost due E of the highest pt. of the mtn. Warden and simple restaurant service, 75 places.

8   From Arolla post office take a signposted track off the N side of the village square, up grassy slopes to a signposted fork in 20 min. Take the R branch (L for Pas de Chèvres) and traverse the pleasant pastures of Pra Gra, passing above this hamlet to reach a group of chalets at pt. 2479m. The path bears L (WNW) and traverses horizontally (water supply channel) into the bed of the Ignes valley). Continue up rocks and grass past pt. 2706m. to resume a traverse to the N, rising steadily all the way to the hut ($2\frac{1}{2}$ h. from Arolla).

<u>Dix Hut</u>   2928m.

LK 1346. Cabane des Dix. SAC. Situated on rocks of the true L bank of the Cheilon gl., and below a knoll called the Tête Noire. One of the largest, busiest and most popular huts in the Alps. Warden, full restaurant service, places for 220.

9   From Val d'Hérémence. Bus service to the Chargeur, Dixence barrage wall terminus. Cableway service (2141-2433m.) to top of barrage. Engineer's road, partly in tunnels, along W side of lake to its end, pt. 2372m. Public motorboat service down entire length of lake; this saves $1\frac{1}{2}$ h. walking on road. At the bottom of the lake there is a bridge (2386m.) over an infall stream at the SW corner. Leave the road and take a track above this bridge which soon turns L (E) and becomes well marked in a rising traverse, turning ESE (Pas du Chat), then S to join moraine above the W side of the Cheilon gl. Follow moraine to the foot of the Tête Noire, move L on to the gl. and continue under the rock promontory until having made a half circle to the R the path goes up to the hut on the most southerly outcrop ($1\frac{1}{2}$ h. from S end of lake).

27

10 From Arolla, over the <u>Pas de Chèvres</u> (2855m.). From the post office take a signposted track off the N side of the village square, up grassy slopes to a fork. Keep straight up (L) to reach a pleasant shoulder where another path joins, coming from the new access road system above Arolla village. Continue past the Kiosses (2330m.) and Remointse (2409m.) chalets by the excellent path W up a broad valley to reach the col at the top ($2\frac{1}{4}$ h., $1\frac{1}{4}$ h. in descent). On the other side descend a short rockface and ledgeline with iron ladder/cables, slanting R to L facing outwards. Reach the dry gl. and cross it SW over moraine heaps, beware of wet boggy sections, to the opposite bank, below the hut perched on some rocks. Turn the rocks on the L and follow a small track to the hut (1 h., 45 min. in reverse; $3\frac{1}{4}$ h. from Arolla, 2 h. in opposite direction).

Prafleuri Hut   2662m.

LK 1326. Marked but not named on map. Privately owned and run, generally open. Situated in the Combe de Prafleuri directly above the Dixence barrage. Places for 40.

11 From the top of the public service cableway (2433m.) at the Dixence barrage, follow a signposted path NW then SW round a shoulder into the Combe. Continue by the good easy angled path to the hut on a knoll above the stream bed (1 h.).

Pantalons Blancs Bivouac   3280m.

LK 1326. Refuge-igloo des Pantalons Blancs. SAC, new in 1975, not marked on map. Situated on a small rock island halfway up a gl. spur dividing the Ecoulaies and Pantalons Blancs gl., and between the Rochers du Bouc (3314.2m.) and the Pte. du Crêt (3323m.). This is almost due W of and above S end of the Dix lake. Door open, no warden, stove, utensils, etc., places for 15.

12 From Val d'Hérémence. Bus service to the Chargeur, Dixence barrage wall terminus. Cable service (2141-2433m.)

to top of barrage. Follow engineer's road through tunnels along W side of lake as far as the Barma stream. About 50 m. before the main stream (bridge) leave the road and ascend R up a small track to the Barma chalet (2458m.). From here climb straight up (SW) towards the Rochers du Bouc, turning the first outcrops on its developing ridge (2768m.) by flanking movements to the L. Return to the crest and follow it over easy rocks to pt. 3089m. Continue up the crest over pt. 3152 and 3256m. to its summit, 3314m., then descend a steep rock ridge with fixed stanchions to a gl. saddle (3230m.). Follow the gl. spur ahead (SW) to the hut a short distance away ($3\frac{1}{2}$-4 h. from top of cableway/barrage wall).

13 From Val de Bagnes, Fionnay village (1489m.). Follow main road SE out of village for 10 min., to a path on the L, going up to the Alpe du Crêt, first in a long series of zigzags in open forest, then at a somewhat easier angle to the chalets. Some 10 min. before the chalets (2298m.) take a L fork to avoid the chalets ($2\frac{1}{4}$ h.). The path climbs E on the L side then the R side of the stream into the cwm bed of the Plan des Lires (2573m.). Trend a little R up broad grass/scree slopes ahead and reach to the R of a moraine spur (2856m.) a small scree hollow (2826m.) below the main ridge S of Le Parrain. Directly above (E) is Col 3150m. This is nearer to the hut than the more frequented Col du Crêt (3144m.) further N. Climb scree, rubble and snow patches to Col 3150m., level on the other side with the Ecoulaies gl. ($2\frac{3}{4}$ h.). Cross the easy gl. almost due E and rise a little on to the gl. spur to reach the hut from above (20 min., about $5\frac{1}{2}$ h. from Fionnay village).

Underline: St. Laurent Hut 2522m.

LK 1326. Marked but not named on map. Property of the Arpettaz Ski Club, door locked, obtain keys from telephone exchange at the artificial Cleuson lake. The hut is above (S of) the end of this lake (2186m.), and should not be confused with the natural Lac de Cleuson (2642m.) further S. Cooking utensils, etc., 35 places.

14 From the Val de Nendaz, limited bus service or taxi, road motorable to the artificial Cleuson lake and along its E bank to roadhead at Les Tsamos (2259m.). Parking. A rough jeep road continues all the way to the hut (parking) via La Gouille then zigzags to the SW. On foot, 1 h.

Mont Fort Hut   2457m.

15 LK 1326. Cabane du Mont Fort. SAC. Situated W of Mt. Fort on a grassy spur below the Monts de Sion, above the Val de Bagnes. Warden and restaurant service, 100 places. Access from Verbier (buses) by the Mt. Gelé cableway system, either by a good path from its Les Ruinettes sta. (2195m.) in $1\frac{1}{2}$ h. or from the higher Les Attelas sta. (2733m.) along a descending traverse path SE in 45 min. The access road from Verbier to La Chaux pastures (2237m.) is forbidden to motorists.

Chanrion Hut   2462m.

LK 1346. Cabane de Chanrion. SAC. Situated at the head of the Val de Bagnes, some distance beyond (S of) the Mauvoisin lake, among grassy knolls and tarns of the Chanrion and Chermotane pastures. Warden, simple restaurant service, 35 places.

16 To Mauvoisin barrage (1841m.), bus service. The road ascends to W side of dam wall and continues down this side of lake, partly tunnelled, to the S end where it becomes a jeep track, limited carparking, $1\frac{3}{4}$ h. on foot. Road exposed to stonefall. Bad avalanches in winter. The jeep road continues but should not be tried by motorists. The excellent path works S above the R side of the infall river which is later crossed L at the Lancet bridge (2040m.). On the other side take a steep zigzag path E and SE, forking L at a junction (2213m.), up to the Chanrion pastures where the path turns R (SE) to reach the hut ($1\frac{3}{4}$ h., $3\frac{1}{2}$ h. from Mauvoisin barrage).

Note: From Vignettes hut, see Rte. 7. For connection across frontier to the Ital. By-Ollomont cwm, see under

30

Fenêtre de Durand, Rtes. 167, 168, 6 h. from Glacier roadhead.

ITALIAN

Aosta Hut   2781m.

LK 1347. Rifugio Aosta. CAI. Situated at the foot of the W ridge of the Tête de Valpelline, and above the E bank of the Tsa de Tsan gl. Places for 18, wood and gas stoves, kitchen utensils, etc., but safer to take your own stove. Water from snowmelt about 100m. away. No permanent warden, door open. Avalanche damage and water infiltration may result in blankets and other articles being stored away in dry cupboards.

17 In the Valpelline the approach has changed and is much longer and more tiring than it used to be. Start from the road-head carpark at Place Moulin (Albergo below), c. 1950m. From here walk along the new path now constructed along the N side of the barrage and at the far end reach the deserted hamlet of Prarayer (2005m.) (1 h.). From here follow the clearly marked path on the L side of the Buthier river to a bridge somewhat above the junction bridge (2021m.) with the stream coming down from the Braoulè gl. cwm to the N. Do not cross this second bridge to the other side of the river (old rte.), despite the fact that all paths shown on maps indicate you should. A few m. before the bridge turn L up a small but clear track with red waymarks which takes you up the L side of the stream, as before. The path is later followed with numerous cairns which peter out on moraines higher up. The hut is soon visible a long way off. Continue by a vague track which later works further away from the river. Gradually in barely recognisable zigzags it climbs L across several streams coming down from the rock barrier supporting the higher Alpe de Tsa de Tsan. Keep working up to the N, tedious, till the huge moraine crest is reached. Follow this to nearly its end (2715m.) against rocks. Now traverse R, steep and loose at first below these

rocks and contour R on to the T sa de Tsan gl. , which is crossed,
icy and loose stones, to the opposite E side. Above, the moraine on which the hut stands is reached at an obvious gap a
short distance below the hut, by climbing a loose and unpleasant
gully containing a stream (4 h. from Prarayer, 5 h. from
Place Moulin).

The original approach by crossing the bridge mentioned above
and following terraces above the R side of the river is still
waymarked with paint and cairns. However it is impossible
to recross the river, either at pt. 2250m. or near pt. 2318m.
(original bridges washed away once too often to be replaced).
Therefore by this rte. you must climb on to the lower tongue
of the Grandes Murailles gl. up to the R (E). Crossing this
in the early 1970s involved about 50m. of steep ice climbing,
requiring crampons and step cutting, in order to rejoin the
original moraine track on this R side of the river.

Bertol - Aosta huts connection (across the Col des Bouquetins)

18 A short connection, not entirely easy but the best way of
going from the Arolla area to the Aosta hut for climbing the
Dent d'Hérens (Pennine Alps Central area). Ital. side, PD-.

From the Bertol hut descend the approach rock staircase to
the gl. and cross snow slopes E to round the rock base
pt. 3229m. Continue over large snowfields SE then S with a
few crevasses to the broad saddle of the Col des Bouquetins
(3357m.) ($1\frac{1}{2}$ h.). On the other side, hardly distinguishable
at first, steer SW for a few min. to the edge of a snow bowl.
Go round the L side of this on to scree along the top of a rock
barrier stretching right along under the pass. Descend as
soon as possible down a convenient snow tongue or gully, at
least 200m. E of pt. 3212m. , on to the Haut Tsa de Tsan gl.
Cross the gl. snowfields SE to the Col de la Division (3314m.),
an obvious opening in the rock barrier on the S side of the gl.
Descend from this col in a steep couloir, rock and snow, where
32

the rte. is variable, but normally best on the R side, down to snow and scree and a few old cairns. A vague cairned track works SW down scree to a series of zigzags through rockbands, then joins moraine and grass above the lower tongue of the Haut Tsa de Tsan gl. It shortly reaches the Aosta hut ($1\frac{1}{4}$ h., $2\frac{3}{4}$ h. from Bertol hut, $3\frac{1}{4}$ h. in reverse direction).

Bouquetins - Aosta huts connection (across the Col du Mt. Brulé)

19 The Col du Mt. Brulé (3213m.) is a pass frequented as part of the High Level Route, which continues to the Col de Valpelline (Pennine Alps Central area). The connection is particularly convenient from the new Bouquetins biv. hut. F+.

From the Bouquetins hut descend S to the gl. and go up the huge snow bay SE to the foot of the col, under and R of the Pte. de la Gde. Arête (3350.5m.) further L (N). About 800m. to the S appears the equally easy looking Col de Tsa de Tsan which must be ignored. From a small bergschrund ascend the top slope of the col, often scree, slanting from R to L. The best crossing place is a short distance S of the lowest pt. of the saddle (1 h.). On the other side, level with the S-most bay of the Haut Tsa de Tsan gl., descend NW in the middle of the slope and reach the lower end of the large gl. terrace lying below the Bouquetins. Contour in a wide arc keeping L (W then N) to below the Col des Bouquetins (crevasses), where the previous rte. is joined near pt. 3212m., and followed over the gl. to the Col de la Division, then down to the hut ($2\frac{1}{4}$ h., $3\frac{1}{4}$ h. from Bouquetins hut).

Col Collon Hut   2818m.

LK 1347. Rifugio Col Collon. CAI. A remote base near the top of the Oren cwm under Col Collon, on a rock spur above the cwm bed. Warden rarely in attendance, door open, wood and gas stoves but no wood in store and safer to take your own stove. Kitchen and cooking utensils, 40 places.

20 From the roadhead carpark at the Place Moulin barrage (c. 1950m.) walk along the new path now constructed along the N side of the lake. Some distance before Prarayer this path crosses the Oren stream and in a few min. reaches La Lé chalet (c. 1990m.) at the end of the lake. Leave the path and go up L (N) behind the chalet along a shoulder enclosing the R side of the Oren stream, which is crossed L by a bridge near the higher Pra Mondzou chalet (2088m.) (1 h.). Now take a track R above the L side of the stream, reaching first Alpe d'Oren (2161m.) then, higher up and by crossing the stream again, the Garda chalet (2211m.). Follow track on the R side of the stream to moraine and a stony plain at the entrance to a gorge at the top, where the valley bends R (1½ h.). Close to the rock barrier on the R, and close to the main stream L, at the upper end of the plain, the track climbs rapidly R (NE) in zigzags up grass shelves and rockbands above the angle of the gorge. The track is poor and vague in places with occasional cairns and eventually reaches a larger marker cairn at the top of this section and above the gorge. In descent, this pt. is quite difficult to find. Cross the stream and follow an inter-mittent track in debris on the L side to a vague fork (straight ahead for Col Collon). Bear up L over rocks and snow patches to the hut on a promontory (1¼ h., 3¾ h. from Place Moulin).

Note: Col Collon - Bouquetins huts connection over Col Collon, see Rte. 4.

COMBA D'OREN Valpelline

Col d'Oren 3262 — 137

Ptes. d'Oren 3490.1 — 77

Col de l' Evêque (concealed) 3525 — 77

L'Evêque 3716.3 — 61 — 3399 — 3465

MT. COLLON

P. Kurz 3498.3 — 56

Mt. Brulé 3585

Col Collon hut

Brulé gl.

136 — 20.

Grandes Dents Chain

The appropriate name given to the chain of rock peaks flanking the E side of the Arolla valley. The S limit is put at the Col de Bertol (hut). The rock is gneiss and generally good, giving a variety of middle grade rock climbs and a few unusual climbs on snow/ice. Nearly all rtes. on the Arolla side can now be started from the Tsa hut.

PETITE DENT DE VEISIVI   3183.6m.

LK 1327. A popular scramble, one of the best training climbs in the Pennine Alps. Nail scratched everywhere. First recorded tourist ascent: A. Tschumi, E. Thury, 8 August, 1885.

South-East (Tsarmine) Ridge (from Col de Tsarmine). The

classic rte., a first rate scramble on perfect rock. III. The traditional approach from the valley (Satarma) on a good track is a stiff pull up. The new approach from the Tsa hut is a long up and down traverse at c. 2700m., mainly trackless and requiring some rte. finding ability at present. First ascent by crest: F. Aston-Binns, O.K. Williamson with J. Maître and a porter, 17 August, 1896.

21 From Arolla descend the main road towards Satarma hamlet. About one km. before Satarma there is a turning on the R over the river to the Pramousse chalets (1835m.). From here take a traverse path L into the forest and continue over a stream to a junction with a mule path coming from the lower hamlet of La Gouille. Now go straight up in many short zigzags to emerge from the forest at pt. 2177m. where the path turns N to reach the Tsarmine chalet (2325m.) (1 h. from main road). The path continues NE, crosses a stream and reaches the grassy cwm below the mtn. The moraines are avoided by

36

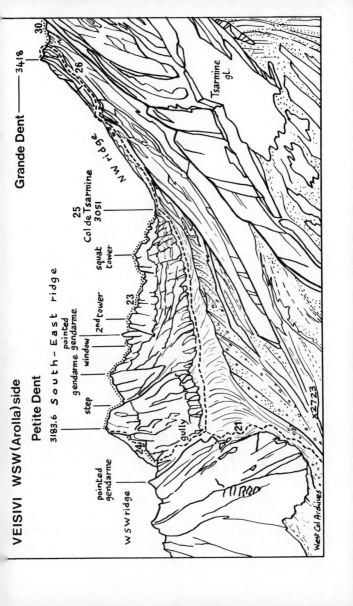

VEISIVI WSW (Arolla) side

Grande Dent ———— 3418

Petite Dent

3183.6 S o u t h - E a s t r i d g e

pointed gendarme

WSW ridge

pointed gendarme

step

window

2nd tower

squat tower

Col de Tsarmine 3051

WNW ridge

Tsarmine gl.

30

26

25

23

21

24

gully

x2723

West Col Archives

keeping close under the S wall of the mtn., curving round easily to the Col de Tsarmine (3051m.) (2 h., $3\frac{1}{2}$-4 h. from Arolla post office).

22 From the Tsa hut go up the saddle behind the hut for a few min. then turn NE and traverse scree/grass slopes in a contouring movement round the first of several shallow cwms divided by old moraine crests and rocky spurs. Pass round the first shoulder above pt. 2619m. and cross a narrow ridge at c. 2720m. descending from the Dent de Perroc. Continue N over rough ground and aim to reach a fairly obvious shoulder at pt. 2707m. From here traverse then descend c. 100m. round a bluff and work below the frontal moraine of the Tsarmine gl., rising a little to join the path of the previous rte. at c. 2620m. ($1\frac{1}{2}$ h.). Continue by this approach to the col (1 h., $2\frac{1}{2}$ h. from Tsa hut).

23 From the col follow the ridge crest with slight detours as necessary over a squat tower then a series of small teeth to a second tower. From the latter descend to a narrow gap in front of a big pointed gendarme. This can be climbed direct by a chimney/crack (IV) but it is normally turned on the R over a series of gangways (III) to rejoin the ridge through a narrow window marking a saddle behind the gendarme. Continue up the crest with short wall pitches (III) to the top of the next gendarme, and descend into the gap beyond. The main step of the summit tower rises above. This can be climbed by pitches of IV but is normally avoided by a rising traverse on the R side where the well marked trail rejoins the crest a few m. from the summit (2 h., 6 h. from Arolla, $4\frac{1}{2}$ h. from Tsa hut).

West-South-West Ridge. The normal descent rte., clearly nail scratched. Indicated on map. II. First ascent: H. Seymour

King, H. Barrett with L. Anthamatten, A. Supersaxo, 29 August, 1885.

24 From the summit descend the ridge for a few m. to a steep chimney cutting the L (S) side. Go down this on excellent holds (II) to ledges and cross these to rejoin the crest. Follow the steep block ridge with interest down to a large saddle with a pointed gendarme beyond. Leave the ridge and descend the well marked trail in rock and grass on the L (S) side, down a gully to join at the bottom (c. 2900m.) the path coming up from the valley in the angle under the S face where the ascent trail traverses E to the Col de Tsarmine (1 h. in descent, $1\frac{1}{2}$ h. in ascent).

COL DE TSARMINE 3051m.

25 LK 1327. Between the Petite and Grande Dent de Veisivi, of no interest as a pass but climbed frequently on the W side for access to its flanking summits. See Rtes. 21, 22. First tourist traverse: J. A. Luttman-Johnson, F. C. Mills with F. Biner, G. Taugwalder, 24 July, 1886.

GRANDE DENT DE VEISIVI 3418m.

LK 1327. This mtn. is of less interest to the average climber than its lower neighbour but is ascended frequently. First ascent: J.S. and Mrs. Philpott with M. Pralong, J. Vuigner, 2 September, 1875.

North-West Ridge (from Col de Tsarmine). The usual rte., pleasant enough and easily combined with the Petite Dent in one day. PD-. First ascensionists.

26 From the Col de Tsarmine (Rtes. 21, 22) climb a snow slope and rocks on the R of the ridge to where the ridge narrows and becomes steep. Take slabs down to the R, loose, then enter and climb a steep icy couloir slanting L to ridge

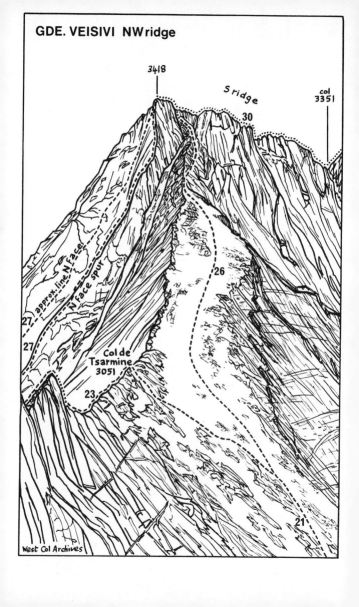

behind the summit. On the crest one short step, simple when dry but greasy if damp, leads to easy scrambling and the top ($1\frac{1}{4}$ h., $5\frac{1}{4}$ h. from Arolla, $3\frac{3}{4}$ h. from Tsa hut).

27 North Face. A remote and serious rte. approached from Les Haudères, half snow, half rock in the main couloir line below the summit. 700m., TD with pitches of V+. F. Hächler, A. Strickler, 3 July, 1960. The rock spur immediately R of this rte. (pt. 2691m.) gives a better, safer and easier climb with some poor rock. 700m., IV+. D. and L. Louvel, 12 August, 1973.

BLANCHE DE PERROC 3651m.

LK 1327. Really the N peak of the Dent de Perroc but with individual rtes. of some character and interest. However, the average mountaineer is warned that it is preferable to reach the summit from the Dent de Perroc. First ascent: J.A. Vardy with J. and P. Maître, 1 September, 1886.

North-West Ridge. Contrary to popular belief this is not an attractive climb although it has the reputation of being the best and simplest rte. The rock is generally poor, in places dangerously so, and if conditions permit snow at the edge of the NW face should be climbed instead. AD-. First ascent: W. Leaf, C. Nettleship, G.W. Prothero with A. Kalbermatten, C. Zurbriggen, 28 July, 1890.

28 From the Tsa hut follow Rte. 22 to just beyond the bluff turned after passing pt. 2707m. Now climb directly up tedious moraine to an opening beside pt. 2839m. leading on to the Tsarmine gl. ($2\frac{1}{2}$ h.). Above is the N spur of the NW ridge. The original rte. crosses the bergschrund and climbs the crest of this N spur to the NW ridge above. The rock is generally loose with pitches of II+. Alternatively and better in good snow conditions, cross the bergschrund further L and climb the

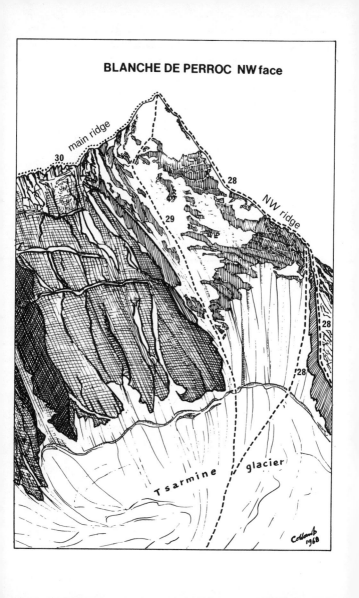

BLANCHE DE PERROC NW face

main ridge

30

NW ridge

29

28

28

28

Tsarmine glacier

Collomb
1968

snow face parallel to and L of the N spur, to reach the NW ridge somewhat higher. Now follow the ridge keeping close to the crest on mixed terrain. The rock sections are steep and near the top so loose as to make it advisable to traverse L up the icy edge of the NW face ($2\frac{1}{2}$ h. , 5 h. from Tsa hut).

North-West Face. An ice climb that needs a lot of snow on it to be safe, and generally not advisable after mid-July. It is the impressive ice wedge at the top of the Tsarmine gl. , immediately L of Rte. 28, with a remote and desolate outlook. Normally bad stonefall in August. According to conditions, D-/D+, 550m. , average angle 53° with steeper sections. First ascent: M. and O. Ebneter, P. Diethelm, 15 July, 1963. In winter: F. Balmer, G. Gobat, J. J. Grimm, M. Zuckschwerdt, 21 January, 1973. Solo: D. Heymans, 19 July, 1973. First British ascent: L. N. Griffin, C. Torrans, July, 1975.

29 From the Tsa hut approach as for Rtes. 22, 28 to pt. 2839m. ($2\frac{1}{2}$ h.). Traverse L below the bergschrund to rocks marking L edge of face. This movement across the Tsarmine gl. can be complicated by a multiple bergschrund system under the face. Cross the bergschrund at the extreme L and climb the snow/ice slope, trending slightly L and working from one outcrop to another. Reach a rock rib on the L and follow its R edge for some way, to where the ice slope steepens. Make a rising traverse R across a zone of smooth slabs which could be very difficult if not well covered with snow. When you are directly below the summit climb straight to the top (6-7 h. from bergschrund).

Blanche de Perroc - Gde. Dt. de Veisivi Main Ridge. This section of the main ridge is the most interesting part of the complete traverse of the Grandes Dents. Its lowest pt. between the two summits is gap 3351m. , which can be reached from the Tsarmine gl. by a deep prominent couloir (PD+, stonefall), so that the ridge could be followed in either direction. The main ridge is described from S to N, being the direction it is most often followed. AD with pitches of III, varied and on mostly good rock (reverse direction, D-, pitches of IV). To gap 3351m.: A. G. Topham with J. and A. Maître, 31 July, 1890. Gap 3351m. to Gde. Dent: J. and W. Outram with J. Maître, 25 August, 1899.

30 From the summit of the Blanche de Perroc follow a fine snow crest. When badly corniced use rocks on the R side. This leads to a series of short steep gendarmes. Keep as close as possible to the sharp crest, climbing over and down a good number of pitches, abseils useful, to reach a small gap behind a big step (3460m.) which drops to gap 3351m. Descend this step by abseiling and climbing round the L (W) side, or descend the rockface on your R which forms the E side of the step ($1\frac{3}{4}$ h.). From gap 3351m. continue on the crest, climbing or turning numerous gendarmes of no special difficulty ($1\frac{3}{4}$ h., 3 h. from Blanche de Perroc to Gde. Dt.).

31 <u>Main Ridge to Dent de Perroc.</u> In either direction very short, a sharp broken crest with a few awkward movements, II+ (15 min.).

DENT DE PERROC 3675.7m.

LK 1327. Sometimes called the Central Peak of the Dents de Perroc, where the N peak of this trio is formed by the Blanche de Perroc and the S and highest peak by the Pte. des Genevois. Its climbs are closely associated with these adjoining summits. First ascent: A. B. Hamilton, W. R. Rickman with J. Anzevui, J. Vuigner, 31 August, 1871.

<u>West-South-West Ridge</u>. The normal rte. and the best way up to the Grandes Dents ridge hereabouts. Also the best descent rte. on the mtn. Climbed frequently. The easiest line where

the rock is fairly good is not simple to find. Pitches of II+/III.
First ascensionists.

32 From the Tsa hut cross the shoulder behind the hut and
make a rising traverse L (NE) up tedious grass and scree to
snow patches in bad debris under the ridge. A rib extends
down from pt. 3046m. Go up the R side of this into a loose
couloir which leads to a gap behind this pt. (1½ h.). Now
follow the broad crest using shallow gullies mainly on the R
side to a step. Turn this on the R and return to the crest as
soon as possible. Reach a chimney of rough red rock which
is climbed on excellent holds to the head of a couloir dropping
to your L. Continue on the R flank of the ridge till the steep
crest can be reached and followed for three rope lengths on
good smooth rock to the summit (2½ h., 4 h. from Tsa hut).
In descent the crest can be followed more directly, abseiling
as required from a number of fixed pegs.

<u>Main Ridge from Pte. des Genevois.</u> Usually the most trouble-
some section of the Grandes Dents main ridge. The rock is
good on the crest but you may be forced off on to the flanks in
bad conditions where the rock is doubtful and from where it
may be difficult to regain the crest. Pitches of III/IV, sustained. First traverse: A. G. Topham with J. Maître, P.
Maurys, 27 July, 1891.

33 From the Pte. des Genevois follow the crest as closely as
possible. Traverse several gendarmes and turn others on
the R (E). III/III+, short abseils useful, especially on the big
exposed descent of the main second gendarme above an obvious
gap and lowest pt. in the ridge. From the gap climb steep
slabs then a gendarme by a series of mantelshelves (III), or
turn it fairly easily on the L (W). The next gendarme is harder; climb direct (III+/IV), or turn it on the L and reach the
foot of the steep summit tower. Climb this by a fine steep

45

knife edge of rock which overhangs the Arolla side (III) ($1\frac{1}{2}$ h.).

South-West Buttress. A fairly well defined buttress rising directly to the summit and flanked by obvious couloirs. A good steep rte. on mainly excellent rock with a well maintained standard. Original, IV. Direct, IV with a short section of V, A1. 450m. First ascent: J. L. Belton, P. J. Graham, T. Kenny, 11 August, 1967. Direct: J. B. Fellay, J. P. Hiroz, 8 August, 1971.

34 From the Tsa hut approach as for Rte. 32 and ascend the laborious stonefield L of pt. 3110m. to snow patches below the buttress and directly in the summit line ($1\frac{1}{2}$ h.).

Original rte. Start at the L side and climb diagonally R over stepped rocks (III) to a prominent chimney/crack cutting the R flank of the buttress, close to its crest line. Climb this in several good pitches for 200m. (III+/IV) to where the chimney divides on reaching a couloir on the R side of the buttress. Exit L (IV) and follow steep slabs and short walls (IV) to the crest line at a pt. where the angle is easier.

Direct rte. Instead of moving R into the chimney/crack, climb the crest line L of it direct (IV) up to an overhanging wall. Start up a crack to the L (A1, V). When the crack becomes too wide for pegging, traverse 2m. R and exit direct (IV), 4 pegs. Continue up the steep and in places strenuous crest (III/III+) with a fine chimney (IV) higher up, to where the angle eases and the crest is joined by the original rte.

Follow the crest (III) to the foot of the summit wall. Make a rising traverse R to the ridge on the R which is reached approx. 20m. from the top (Rte. 33). Climb the final ridge by a fine steep rock knife edge which overhangs the Arolla side (III) (3-4 h. from foot of buttress).

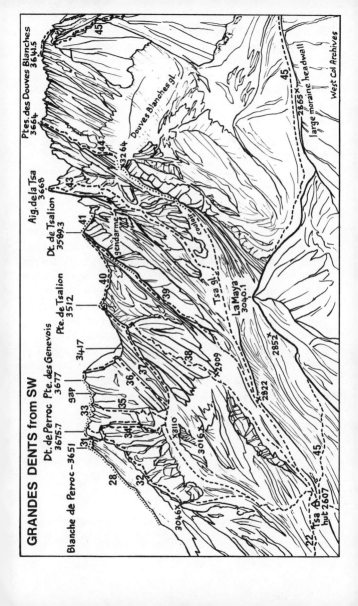

GRANDES DENTS from SW

Blanche de Perroc – 3651
Dt. de Perroc Pte. des Genevois
3675.7 3677
Pte. de Tsalion
3512
Dt. de Tsalion
3599.3
Aig. de la Tsa
3668
Ptes. des Douves Blanches
3664.5
3664

Douves Blanches gl.

3264

44I

43

4I

40

gendarme

couloir

39

Tsa gl.

La Maya
3040.1

2852×

2822

+2909

×2852

38

34I7

9ar

37

36

35

33

34

3IIO

3016×

28

3I

32

3046×

22

Tsa

hut 2607

45

45

2865×I

large moraine headwall

West Col Archives

<u>West-South-West (Carougeois) Buttress</u>. The obvious buttress R of the SW one, descending from a gendarme on the main ridge (Rte. 33) midway between the Dt. de Perroc and Pte. des Genevois. This gendarme is the one above the lowest gap in the ridge. A good rock climb of uneven difficulty with pitches of IV, IV+ and one of V, A1. 450m. First ascent: C. Stucki with J. B. Fellay, 9 October, 1971.

35 Approach as for the SW buttress, from the base of which the start is c. 120m. further R. In the line of the buttress crest climb an initial zone of easy-angled slabs, followed by a sweep of steeper slabs. The best way up the latter is a zig-zag line between short steps; several smooth bits with friction moves and pegs for protection (IV+). Finish on easier rock under a large red wall. Climb the wall by a fine vertical dièdre (V, A1, 8 pegs, one wedge), followed by two pitches of IV (2 pegs) which lead to the end of major difficulties. Follow the upper crest of the buttress (II, III) to the top of the gendarme on the main ridge where Rte. 33 is joined (4-5 h. from foot).

Note: When coming from the midway gendarme local guides appear to use a traverse line below the crest of the main ridge, on the Arolla side, to reach the WSW ridge of the Dt. de Perroc. This traverse does not exceed II and appears to take a line some 30-40m. below the crest, and descends the exit of the SW buttress (before it finishes up the main ridge), then almost immediately works L (W) on to the upper part of the WSW ridge.

POINTE DES GENEVOIS   3677m.

LK 1327, 1347. The southerly and highest pt. of the Dents de Perroc and of the Grandes Dents as a whole. A popular climb. First ascent: W. Kündig, A. Tschumi with J. Quinodoz, 22 July, 1885.

<u>South Ridge</u>. The normal rte., quite interesting. PD+ with

pitches of III. First ascensionists.

36 From the Tsa hut cross the shoulder behind the hut and make a rising traverse L (NE) up tedious grass and scree to the large stonefield descending from below the SW-W face of the Perroc summits. Climb straight up and L of a promontory (3110m.) to a snow slope below and well R of the summit line, under three buttresses coming down NW from the main ridge.

Climb into a couloir between the second and third buttresses, counting from the R (S) (2 h.). Snow and scree in the bed is followed by chimney and slab pitches rising into a steep nose which peters out into a sweep of cracked slabs. Climb these (III) to the main ridge (45 min.). In conditions of stonefall, there is a safer and easier line on a rib L of gully. Go along the level ridge, either over small teeth on the crest or just R of them to where the crest steepens. Climb a fine steep chimney just R of crest on perfect rock, and continue by the airy crest, turning a pinnacle on its L, to the summit (1 h., $3\frac{3}{4}$ h. from Tsa hut).

Traverse of the Dents de Perroc (Main Ridge). A classic expedition, nowadays much facilitated by the Tsa hut. Comparable with the Aigs. Rouges traverse, though shorter and less serious than the Bouquetins and Singla traverses. From S to N is much the best way. D-. Combine Rtes. 36, 33, 31, 30 and descend by 26. Tsa hut to Col de Tsarmine, $8\frac{1}{2}$ h. without halts.

POINTE DE TSALION 3512m.

37 LK 1347. An undistinguished summit on the main ridge between the Pte. des Genevois and Dent de Tsalion, rarely climbed for itself. Easily climbed from the entry couloir of Rte. 36 by moving R (S) under the face and taking a large scree/snow band which slants diagonally from L to R across the W flank to the summit (about 3 h. from Tsa hut).

<u>West Face Pillar</u>. A varied climb on excellent rock with a well maintained standard. 600m. IV+. First ascent: D. and L. Louvel, 25 August, 1972.

38 From the Tsa hut follow the shoulder behind the hut for a few min. then traverse R under rocks of the continuation spur above. Go up moraine and snow in the bed on the R (S) side of the spur to the lowest pt. (2909m.) of the W face, directly below the summit (1 h. or less).

Start 50m. L of the lowest pt. and climb a grassy ledge system R to large slabs in a direct line. Take these (II) to black slabs higher. Turn these on the L by climbing a slanting couloir for 80m. , then follow another couloir diagonally R (III) to the crest line, at the foot of a pillar. Get on to a large terrace above. Climb the first wall by a short traverse L and a few m. direct to a stance on the R (IV). Traverse 5m. L and mount a block below a large dièdre. Take the dièdre for 10m. then reach the crest on your L (IV). Above, turn a yellow wall on the L and return R immediately (IV+, peg). Now climb a short wall (IV+, peg), traverse L up a slab and avoid an overhang on its L side, then traverse R to a terrace (IV). Above, climb a cracked overhang (V, peg) and follow the crest, turning a gendarme on the L, up to scree bands leading to the summit (IV, IV+) ($4\frac{1}{2}$ h. from foot).

DENT DE TSALION   3589.3m.

LK 1347.   A fairly popular climb, equally approachable from the Tsa or Bertol huts. First ascent: probably A. Cust with F. Biner, 11 August, 1875.

<u>West Ridge</u>. One of the best rock scrambles in the Arolla district, steep and mostly on perfect gneiss. Variable pitches but the crest line should be followed as far as possible. A rte. of character, free from stonefall, easier and less

complicated than the W face of the Tsa, for which it provides
a suitable alternative for reaching that summit. Numerous
pitches of II+ and bits of III. 650m. First ascent: Miss E.
M. L. Wood with J. Maître, P. Maurys, 6 August, 1897.

39 From the Tsa hut cross the shoulder behind the hut, traverse R (S) for 15 min. over steep grassy ground, then climb
SE in a moraine hollow running up to a big moraine ridge on
the R, which leads to the foot of the ridge at c. 2920m. in a
large V corner (1 h.).

From the lowest rock toe move R and ascend a ledge line R
to reach a gully. Ascend this briefly then exit R along narrow
ledges rising R. Continue on the ridge flank trending L up
slabs and a crack to reach the crest above its initial steepness.
Follow the ridge on or near the crest with steep rock giving
mainly slab and crack pitches of no particular difficulty and
some choice for 400m., up to a steep little step which occurs
beside the figure 8 in the LK25 map height of the mtn. This
can be climbed direct at grade IV+, but is normally turned on
L by a rising traverse over smooth slabs with poor belays in
two run outs of III. Return to the crest above the step by a
long slabby chimney pitch, variable (III), and continue to the
top on loose but fairly easy rock (4-5 h., 5-6 h. from hut).
The connection for continuing the ascent to reach and climb
the Tsa is the last part of Rte. 41 in reverse.

Main North Ridge to Pte. de Tsalion. This is the best and
quickest descent to the Tsa hut. PD with short pitches of II.

40 Descend the narrow ridge over two or three short steps
with chimney/crack pitches to blocks and loose stones which
soon relent to a broader ridge. Continue easily on scree and
snow to the Pte. de Tsalion (45 min.). From here descend
the large scree/snow band to the N and join Rte. 36 (complete
descent to Tsa hut, $2\frac{1}{4}$ h.).

The easiest rte., a short outing from the
Bertol hut. PD-. The approach is the same as for the Tsa.

41 From the Bertol hut descend to the Col de Bertol then work
NE across the upper snowfield of the Mt. Miné gl., passing
under the SE face of the Pte. de Bertol, then climbing obliquely
R up a snow/rock slope (track) to a narrow saddle in the E
spur of the Pte. de Bertol, above pt. 3372.7m. Descend a
little on the other side and pass close to the Col de la Tsa
(3308m.). Cross the Aiguille gl. due N, sometimes badly
crevassed, to the E foot of the Aig. de la Tsa ($1\frac{3}{4}$ h.). Trend
R and cross a small snow plateau further N, to reach the SE
foot of the Dt. de Tsalion (15 min.). Climb an easy flank of
rocks and snow to the summit (15 min., $2\frac{1}{4}$ h. from Bertol
hut).

AIGUILLE DE LA TSA   3668m.

LK 1347. An attractive pinnacled peak, easily the most popular rock climb in the Arolla district. The E flank stands
only 80m. above the gl. snowfields but the W (Arolla) face is
nearly 700m. high. First ascent: P. Beytrison, G. Gaspoz,
P. Quinodoz, J. and P. Vuigner, 21 July, 1868.

East Flank. The ordinary rte., assailed by all and sundry.
A short slab climb with chimney work to finish, suitable for
half a day. Excellent rock. PD with pitches of III/III+. First
ascensionists.

42 From the Bertol hut follow Rte. 41 to the E base of the peak
($1\frac{3}{4}$ h.). Climb on to the slabby rocks at their NE foot, where
the rock is polished. Ascend trending L then more of a rising
traverse L up a trail of nail scratches. At the top of this slab
section cross a steep smooth slab (III-) to a shoulder/corner.
Now climb direct towards the summit up two short chimneys
which lead to a third chimney (5m., III/III+). Finish with a

short scramble (30 min., $2\frac{1}{4}$ h. from Bertol hut).

West (Arolla) Face. A classic climb with a reputation for stonefall and overrating of difficulties. A lot of parties lose the way, or do not take the most satisfactory line. Many variations are possible, generally on less good rock further R, where you are exposed to stonefall. Generally excellent rock on the proper rte. with continuous pitches of II, III and some of III+/IV. 650m. First ascent: Miss K. Richardson with J. B. Bich, A. Maître, E. Rey, 26 July, 1889.

43 From the Tsa hut approach as for Rte. 39. Bear R (SE) along the moraine rim under the W ridge of the Tsalion and reach snow/rubble round the base of the Tsa at c. 3000m. ($1\frac{1}{4}$ h.). Start 50m. R of the lowest pt., almost in the couloir entrance further R (stonefall). Climb R up broken rock and debris ledges for a few min., then bear L up scree towards a snow patch at the base of the first steep rocks. At the R edge of the snow patch, and on the crest, climb steep, sound but broken rocks trending R up a triangular facet to a vague crest line on the R. Almost immediately climb trending R at a steep angle away from the crest line and below a fine slender gendarme on the crest higher up. Above the level of this, climb in the same line below the crest to a pt. some 30m. below a conspicuous light-coloured wall. Many parties have come out of the snow gully to the R (dangerously) and up rocks direct to this pt. Make a rising traverse R and climb three couloir/ chimneys. The upper "brown" one is IV. Reach a snow/scree patch in a corner about 40m. below the ridge crest. Climb trending R up a fine staircase pitch (40m., III) to a break near another snow patch to the R. Up to the L is a wide crack cutting a pock-marked wall: Passage des Chevilles. Climb this (III+) and at the top continue up steep slabs to a pinnacle on the face, which is turned on the L. Climb across a smooth adjoining slab (IV) to reach a tiny ledge on the L. Now trend R up the face and reach the main ridge at a notch near the foot of the third chimney on Rte. 42. By trending R and traversing R above the Chevilles section, the ridge can be reached at a lower level, at the top of the slab section on Rte. 42. This variation is easier but exposed and sensational (4 h., $5\frac{1}{4}$ h. from Tsa hut).

POINTE NORD DES DOUVES BLANCHES   3664m.

LK 1347. Sometimes climbed from the Bertol hut, fairly easily from the approach of Rte. 42, up rocks and snow on the E side just R of the summit line. More interest as a traverse from the Tsa hut to Bertol hut, going up the W ridge. First ascent: A. Cust, A.H. Cawood, J.B. Colgrove, 17 July, 1874.

<u>West Ridge</u>. An excellent general mountaineering rte., sound rock on its steep upper pitches, and technically the easiest way of reaching the Tsa from the Tsa hut. The descent on the E side to the Aiguille gl. is about 170m. PD with short pitches of II+. First ascent: C.H. Brook, W.A. Gillett with J. Georges, 28 August, 1905.

44 From the Tsa hut approach as for Rtes. 39, 43 and continue S under the W face of the Tsa to below the big couloir separating the Tsa and Douves Blanches ($1\frac{1}{4}$ h.). On the far S side of this climb diagonally L over steep snow to a series of broken rock ribs divided by long snow strips. Climb these fairly steeply to a level saddle at the foot of the ridge proper (c. 3280m.) (45 min.). Go up the ridge on broken rocks, steep in places but generally easy, to a narrow snowband extending L. At this pt. climb the ridge keeping slightly R (S) to a section of mixed ground running up to the final steep crest. Take the crest direct with one fine pitch up a sharp leaf to the summit ($2\frac{1}{4}$ h., $4\frac{1}{4}$ h. from Tsa hut).

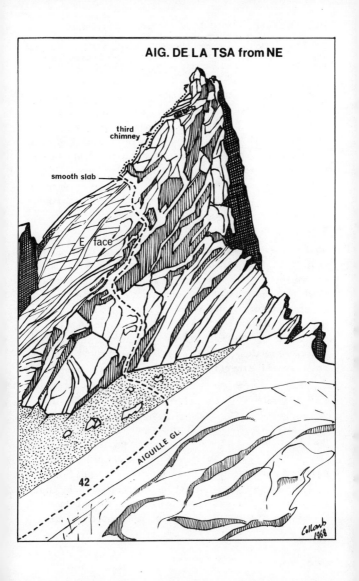

AIG. DE LA TSA from NE

third chimney

smooth slab

E face

AIGUILLE GL.

42

Collomb
1968

LK 1347.   No interest as a summit but renowned for the high
quality rock climb provided by its SW ridge, the Douves Blanches
proper.   First tourist ascent, as Pte. N above.

<u>South-West Ridge</u>.   The longest and most difficult of the popular
rock climbs on the Grandes Dents.   The ridge can be reached
at several pts., but there is not much time to be saved by
starting as high as possible.   The approach from the Tsa hut
is no shorter and much more tedious than the original Bertol
pathway.   The rock is generally excellent.   Pitches of IV with
one long serious pitch of IV+.   About 1500m. of climbing.   In
1975 the rte. was completely depegged except for one pin in
the crux pitch.   First ascent: F. W. Oliver with P. Maître and
a porter, 1 September, 1892.

45 From Arolla start as for Rte. 2 and reach the upper Plan
de Bertol (2664m.) (2h.).   Descend N, cross the Bertol stream
and on the far side climb grass and scree to the foot of the
ridge.   In the R (S) flank climb a couloir/chimney to reach
the crest immediately behind pt. 2891.3m. (45 min.).   Follow
the easy crest over pt. 3037m. to a gap at the foot of a red
cone gendarme (3107m.), about 50m. high.   Climb the crest
to a steep section, which is avoided on the R (III).   Rejoin the
crest beyond the top of the gendarme and follow it to the foot of
a large tower, La Quille (3242m.).   Climb using alternately
slabs immediately R of the crest, and on the crest itself, to a
notch at the foot of a vertical pitch.   Climb the smooth wall
which normally has large fixed pegs in place (IV), and reach
the almost horizontal knife edge which forms the top of La
Quille (2h.).   From the notch at the foot of the peg pitch it is
possible to turn the tower on the L by traversing bad rock.

First alternative start: Reach the foot of La Quille by climbing further up towards the Bertol hut, then crossing the valley
to reach the S flank of the ridge at a pt. somewhat L of a straight

line up to the tower. In the flank, climb a chimney with a large chockstone, or take another chimney further R in a large yellow wall below La Quille. So reach the notch below the peg pitch (III) (1½ h.).

Second alternative start: As for the first alternative, till you are about 50m. below the notch. Slant R across large grey slabs, making a rising traverse at their weakest pt., fairly low, and so turn La Quille and reach the far end of its knife edge (III). By this var. the tower may also be turned when coming up the ridge crest.

Approach from Tsa hut. Cross steep and tedious grass, scree and moraine bands due S, aiming to reach the slopes below La Maya at c. 2750m. Now make a rising traverse up an obvious stone shoot which reaches the ridge E of La Maya at c. 2980m. On the other side continuing traversing scree then a large moraine headwall, quite well marked, which on the far S side (2900m.) joins a steep scree inlet cutting the side of the Douves Blanches ridge below pt. 3107m. Climb steep rough ground to the gap before this pt., the red cone gendarme mentioned above, where the rte. on the ridge proper is joined (2½ h.).

From La Quille, a staircase on the ridge leads pleasantly to a cock's comb section. Cross this (III) to a saddle below a huge square shaped tower capped by a large block, the Red Tower. Ways round it are hardly less difficult than the normal procedure of climbing it by three fine short pitches of IV. From the top abseil into the next gap (2 h.), and so reach up slabs the foot of the next large step, the Grey Tower. This overlooks a sweep of grey slabs on the R side (15 min.). Descend about 12m. on the L side to a horizontal ledge of pale rock. Follow this L to a flake crack which leads nicely to the foot of a chimney, the crux. The lower part is narrow, opening higher up into a dièdre with bulges at two or three pts. (30m., IV+, pegs usually in place, sometimes verglassed).

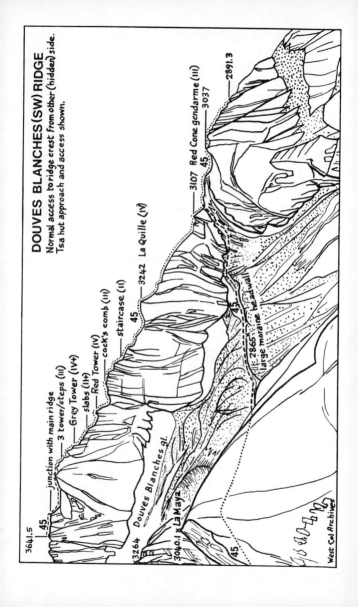

DOUVES BLANCHES (SW) RIDGE

Normal access to ridge crest from other (hidden) side.
Tsa hut approach and access shown.

3641.5
45
junction with main ridge
3 tower/steps (II)
Grey Tower (IV+)
slabs (II+)
Red Tower (IV)
cock's comb (III)
staircase (II)
45
3242 La Quille (IV)
45
3107 Red Cone gendarme (III)
45
3037
2891.3

Douves Blanches gl.

3264
3040.1 La Maya
45

2865
large moraine headwall
45

West Col Archives

The traverse and dièdre pitch have suffered some rockfall changes but was climbed in 1975 without any notable difficulty. It is however possible to climb the ridge direct, up a steep wall and slab, then a short traverse R (V) to a niche below pegs in a cracked overhang. Climb it using the pegs to exit either up a groove L (IV) or a chimney R (IV).

Having rejoined the crest (1 h.), the difficulties ease progressively. Follow it over three smaller tower/steps (III) to snow and large blocks which lead to the main ridge (7-9 h. from Arolla or Tsa hut, according to rte. and conditions).

Descent: Climb down the E flank and soon reach the approach on snow crossed by Rte. 41 (1 h. to Bertol hut).

COL DE LA TSA   3308m.

LK 1347. Between the Douves Blanches S summit and the Pte. de Bertol, a simple gl. pass rarely frequented because of the neighbouring Col de Bertol/hut.

POINTE DE BERTOL   3499m.

LK 1347. A minor pt. behind the Bertol hut, rarely climbed; not easy.

Grandes Dents Complete Traverse

From the Bertol hut to the Col de Tsarmine with possibly the addition of the Petite Dent de Veisivi, or vice versa. A very long expedition of no great technical difficulty but needing a fit and competent party to accomplish it in one day. Not often done. It is questionable whether parties actually pass along the ridge section forming the Douves Blanches summits, or avoid them by Rte. 41, finishing or starting with the Tsa. First complete traverse N-S (Col de Tsarmine to Bertol hut):

59

Miss D. E. Pilley, I. A. Richards, July, 1927. First winter traverse S-N (to Col de Tsarmine): A. Georges, 17-18 March, 1973.

Bouquetins - Brulé Chain

This section of ridge encloses the Haut Arolla gl. on its E and S sides and consists of two principal mtn. groups which have little in common.

COL DE BERTOL   3269m.

LK 1347. Between the Pte. de Bertol and Pte. de la Crête du Plan, an access pass on the high level rte. from Arolla to Zermatt. See Rte. 2. First tourist traverse: A. W. Moore, H. Walker with J. Anderegg, 8 July, 1865.

POINTE DE LA CRÊTE DU PLAN   3374.4m.

46 LK 1347. The SW ridge of this rock pt., immediately S of and easily accessible from the Bertol hut, gives a splendid rock climb of grade III, several abseils necessary. The ridge is attainable at several pts. A fit party with moderate loads can climb it all the way from the bottom as an alternative to Rte. 2 (allow 5-7 h. for ridge). First ascent of ridge thus: E. Carr, F. W. Oliver, Misses C. & M. Pasteur, C. H. Pasteur, C. Wilson with A. Georges, P. Maître, 13 September, 1892.

DENTS DE BERTOL   N. 3547m.   S. 3524m.

47 LK 1347. Fairly prominent rock pts. on the main ridge gathering itself before rising to the Bouquetins. Easily climbed from the col 3416m. between the two main summits. First recorded ascent: J. G. Addenbrook, A. Barran, F. J. Corbett with J. Quinodoz, 13 August, 1886.

BOUQUETINS   3838m.

LK 1347. A magnificent mini-range of rock peaks orientated

N-S which can be traversed to make an expedition which is longer and more serious than either of the usual traverses of the Gds. Dents or Aigs. Rouges. It is lacking only in great height to rank among the finest rock traverses in the Alps. This expedition has been simplified by the construction of the Bouquetins biv. hut. The various distinct peaks formed along the ridge are usually climbed individually and are described as separate rtes. Rock on the W side of the ridge is generally loose and this side, while climbed many times towards the Central and S Peaks, is often raked by stonefall. Rock on the E side is better but tends to verglas quickly. The main ridge from Pte. Barnes, over the S and Central Peaks, to the Col des Dents des Bouquetins, is generally excellent, and to the N Peak and beyond that less good, even bad in places.

Principal first ascents. Central Peak (3838m.): A. B. Hamilton with J. Anzevui, J. Vuigner, 6 September, 1871. Described by Hamilton as a "second class peak", a remark prompted by a dispute with Arthur Cust who, having made the second ascent in 1876, cast doubt based on guides' gossip as to whether Hamilton actually bothered to tread the highest rocks.

North Peak (3779m.): F. A. Monnier with J. Quinodoz, 8 August, 1884. South Peak (3670m.): A. G. Topham with J. Maître, P. Maurys, 18 July, 1894. Pointe Barnes (3612m.): G. S. Barnes, Miss B. Oliphant, W. C. Slingsby with M. Vuigner, 30 August, 1887.

BOUQUETINS NORTH PEAK   3779m.

<u>South Ridge (from Col des Dents des Bouquetins)</u>. Ordinarily the easiest way up, but there is no exact rte. to the col between the N and Central Peaks. The E face of the Central Peak is streaked by thin ice couloirs and ribs, and when the gl. couloir below the col is in bad condition the alternative is to take a line up the E face L of the couloir, according to conditions found, i.e. as for the normal rte. to Central Peak. Mixed climbing, some loose rock, AD-. First ascent: H.S. King with L. Anthamatten, A. Supersaxo, 1 September, 1885.

48 From the Bertol hut or Aosta hut reach the large gl. plateau W of the Col des Bouquetins by Rte. 18 (1½ or 2 h.). Move up the plateau W to a large bergschrund under the broad gl. couloir facing NE and coming down from the col (3675m.). Normally cross the schrund near pt. 3408m., sometimes with difficulty but usually straightforward in early season. According to conditions, climb the gl. couloir keeping R to the col at the top; frequently icy. Alternatively, trend L to rocks and climb these up the L side of the gl. couloir to a general steepening halfway up, where the rocks extend R. Move R and climb diagonally R over the upper gl. couloir to the col ($1\frac{1}{4}$ h.).

From the col climb a steep ridge by the crest with short steps, over a gendarme, then descend to cross another gendarme followed by a steeper descent with loose rock into a deep gap. Climb straight out and trend L to turn the top of a gendarme/step (3750m.), continuing on the ridge up two wide chimneys to a forepeak, a slight gap, then the top of the N Peak ($1\frac{1}{2}$ h., $4\frac{1}{4}$ h. from Bertol hut, $4\frac{3}{4}$ h. from Aosta hut).

North-West Flank and Ridge. A steep snow/ice climb with a nice rock ridge to finish, recommended when conditions are good. AD with a pitch of III+. Descended by H. A. Beeching, H. W. Reade, L. W. Rolleston with A. Bovier father & son, 22 July, 1899.

49 From the Bertol hut start as for Rte. 48 and slant easily R (SW) into the snow cwm leading to a col marked pt. 3448m. (1 h.). Just before the col, bear L, cross a bergschrund, often large, and climb a steep snow/ice slope direct, which is L of the lower snowy part of the ridge. Higher up trend R on to a snow/ice boss formed at c. 3600m. on the ridge. Continue up a fine snow crest, soon steepening into the terminal rock crest. Go up this direct on sound rock giving a variety of pitches including a 10m. step of III+ to the summit ($2\frac{3}{4}$ h., $3\frac{3}{4}$ h. from Bertol hut).

BOUQUETINS CENTRAL PEAK 3838m.

East Flank. See preamble to Rte. 48. The easiest way up the mtn. The ribs and couloirs of the E flank converge at a

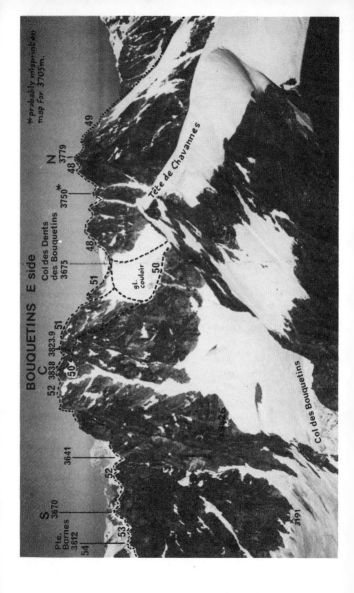

BOUQUETINS E side

S
Pte.
Bornes
3612
3670
54 53
3641
52
52 3838 3823.9 51
C
50 51
48 51
50
gl.
couloir

Col des Dents
des Bouquetins
3675
3750*
48

N
48 1
3779
49

Tête de Chavannes

Col des Bouquetins

2191

*probably misprinted on
map for 3705m.

forepeak pinnacle on the N ridge at pt. 3823.9m. This flank can be climbed almost anywhere L of the gl. couloir descending from the Col des Dents des Bouquetins and a rte. is chosen according to conditions found. Verglassed rock is not infrequent. PD+/AD-. First ascensionists.

50 From the Bertol or Aosta huts reach the large gl. plateau W of the Col des Bouquetins by Rte. 18 ($1\frac{1}{2}$ or 2 h.). Move up the plateau W to a large bergschrund under the broad gl. couloir facing NE and coming down from the Col des Dents des Bouquetins (3675m.). Normally cross the schrund near pt. 3408m., sometimes with difficulty but usually straightforward in early season. Climb trending L up rocks at the L side of the gl. couloir, cross the head of one or two ice gullies, to where the rock edge slants R and steepens at c. 3600m.

Traverse L across a steep narrow ice gully (stonefall) to reach a continuation rib line. Follow this on good rock up slabs and over several small towers and pinnacles, to the rocks immediately below the forepeak (3823.9m.). Traverse L, crossing a couloir, sometimes tricky, and on the far side climb steeply L over mixed ground to the main summit. Alternatively, continue by two steep pitches to the forepeak, then descend 50m. to a deep gap and reach the summit over a step with sloping holds; this is the most reliable way, pitches of II+ ($2\frac{1}{2}$ h., 4 h. from Bertol hut, $4\frac{1}{2}$ h. from Aosta hut).

North Ridge (from Col des Dents des Bouquetins). Really only a variation of Rte. 50. See preambles to Rtes. 48, 50. This section of the main ridge is important in the complete traverse, and as a way to the summit of the Central Peak is no less reliable than the E flank. PD+. First ascent: H.S. King with L. Anthamatten, A. Supersaxo, 1 September, 1885.

51 Reach the Col des Dents des Bouquetins (3675m.) as for Rte. 48. Above the col climb the first big gendarme by its crest and turn its summit on the L. Descend to a gap, which can also be reached directly from below, without going to the col. Climb a number of short steps, making occasional movements on the L (E) side, and so reach the forepeak (3823.9m.). Descend 50m. into a deep gap and reach the summit over a step with sloping holds (1¼ h., 4 h. from Bertol hut, 4½ h. from Aosta hut).

<u>Ridge from South Peak.</u> The S Peak is often the pt. where traverse parties turn back in adverse conditions, although the hardest technical pitch is behind them. See Rte. 53. This portion up to the Central Peak carries about 20 gendarmes, of which 3 are large and the others quite small. The rock is nearly excellent everywhere and the situations are exposed and fine. Numerous pitches of III with moves of III+. First ascent: I. A. Richards with J. Georges, 21 July, 1925.

52 From the S Peak (3670m.) follow crest over various gendarmes until a 30m. gendarme is taken by its edge, soon followed by a large double tower about 25m. high, from where an exposed descent of 50m. leads into a gap (3641m.). Ascend directly up a step to a series of 4 gendarmes and traverse these to where the ridge merges into a facet forming a big step defending the summit. Make a slightly descending traverse R (E) for 75m. below the step, then climb into a very steep chimney which is followed for a long pitch to a break. Traverse up to the R and reach a second chimney which leads more easily to loose broken rock. Ascend direct to a rock head and continue on the crest over a little gap to the summit (3-3½ h.).

SOUTH PEAK or PETIT BOUQUETIN 3670m.

Rarely climbed for itself, there are a number of unsatisfactory rtes. on loose rock up the E and W flanks of this peak. The easiest rte. starts from the Aosta hut and takes the E flank above the Tsa de Tsan gl. The main ridge from Pte. Barnes is described below as part of the traverse to the Central Peak.

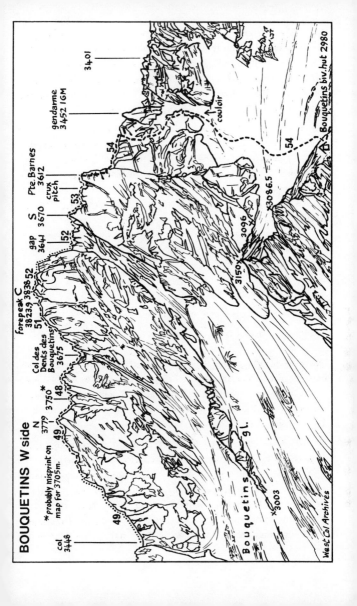

BOUQUETINS W side

col
3448

N 3779
* 3750

* probably misprint on
map for 3705m.

49

48

Col des
Dents des
Bouquetins
3675

49

Forepeak C
3823.9 3838.52

51

52

gap
3644

52

S
3670

53

Pte. Barnes
3612

crux
pitch

53

54

gendarme
3452 IGM

3401

couloir

54

Bouquetins bivy hut 2980

3150

3096

X3086.5

Bouquetins gl.

X3003

West Col Archives

<u>Main Ridge from Pointe Barnes</u>. Though short, the most difficult section of the main ridge traverse to the Central Peak. The crest is cut by small gaps and gendarmes, and has a notably difficult step. A good safe rte. for experienced rock climbers. Pitches of III+ and one of V-. First ascent: I. A. Richards with J. Georges, 21 July, 1925.

53 From Pte. Barnes (3612m.), see Rte. 54, descend cracked slabs in two short pitches then cross a gap to traverse several small gendarmes leading to a good ledge and belay at the foot of a vertical blunt corner/arête at an obtuse angle. Climb this direct on tiny holds (12-15m., V-), with the crux halfway up at a bulge which is turned slightly R, to reach better finishing holds and a large platform. Difficult for pegging and in any case this practice is frowned upon. Continue into a gap and climb near the crest, turning short difficulties, not easily, on the L, to reach the S Peak ($1\frac{1}{4}$ h. from Pte. Barnes).

POINTE BARNES 3612m.

Previously a remote summit and the first obstacle on the traverse of the main Bouquetins ridge to the Central Peak. Now easily approached from the new hut.

<u>South-West Flank and South Ridge</u>. The normal and easiest rte. to reach the Bouquetins ridge from the W side. Some loose rock and stonefall danger on the flank before the crest is reached. PD+ with pitches of II+. First ascensionists of Pte. Barnes.

54 From the Bouquetins biv. hut traverse E on rock and moraine to the snow bay rising into the S side of Pte. Barnes. Go up to a bergschrund below an obvious couloir descending from below a conspicuous gendarme (3452m. IGM) with a flat cap rock on the S ridge of the peak, about 200m. N of pt. 3401m. Cross the sometimes difficult bergschrund and climb the couloir on snow and rock, steepening and narrowing higher up (stonefall). About one third way up trend L up a steep loose ramp in slabby rock, followed by several chimneys with loose blocks (II), trending L to the R end of a prominent snowband high on the ridge flank. Ascend this L for a pitch to its highest pt., then go up broken rock directly to the crest which is reached at the top of a little ridge step above the gap which follows the flat cap gendarme. A sharp but straightforward edge leads to a broader but steeper section taken direct (II) to a large stony platform below the summit step of Pte. Barnes. Traverse L over steep rock with good ledges/holds to a series of chimneys and cracks rising in steps up the W side. Climb these somewhat strenuously in 3 pitches (II+) to a slab split by a crack which leads to the top ($3\frac{1}{4}$ h. from biv. hut).

Bouquetins Complete Traverse. A long, classic rte., now shortened by the Bouquetins biv. hut. Nevertheless, great length combined with fairly sustained difficulties and some-times verglassed rocks make it one of the most serious under-takings in the Western Pennines. Nearly always traversed S to N. Grade: D, with many pitches of III, a few of III+ and one of V-. From Bouquetins biv. hut to Central Peak by Rtes. 54, 53, 52 (8 h.). Continued to N Peak and descent to Bertol hut by Rtes. 51, 48, 49 (5 h., 13 h. without halts; has been done in 8 h.). First traverse: I. A. Richards with J. Georges, 21 July, 1925.

COL DES BOUQUETINS 3357m.

LK 1347. A frontier gl. pass between the Tête Blanche (Tête de Chavannes spur, 3670.6m.) and the Bouquetins, from the Bertol to Aosta huts. See Rte. 18. First traverse: K. E. Digby, W. E. Hall with F. Biner, late August, 1862. In winter on ski: M. Kurz with M. Crettaz, 27 January, 1920.

COL COLLON SW side

3138.6   col (concealed)   La Vierge 3312.2   5   3098

3263.1

56   2989

3498.3   J. P. KURZ   3401

Comba d'Oren

5   Col Collon hut

COL DU MONT BRULÉ   3213m.

LK 1347.   A classic col on the original High Level Route. A
barely distinguishable saddle in the frontier ridge between the
Pte. de la Gde. Arête and rock pt. 3291.7m. Sometimes confused with the Col de Tsa de Tsan, situated S of pt. 3291.7m.
See Rte. 19.   First traverse: E. E. Bowen, C.H. Pilkington,
Sir G. Young with J. V. Favret, B. Nägeli, M. Payot, 11 August, 1862. In winter on ski: M. Baujard with E. D. & J. Rav-
anel, January, 1908.

COL DE TSA DE TSAN   3243m.

55 LK 1347. Situated over one km. S of the Col du Mt. Brulé
(see above), an easy pass but unpleasantly loose and exposed
to stonefall on the Ital. side. See Rte. 57 for access on Swiss
side. First traverse: T. Blanford, E. P. Rowsell, 12 August,
1863.

MONT BRULÉ   3585m.

LK 1347.   Sometimes Mt. Braoulè.   A dromedary mass of
rock and ice forming on the Swiss side the SE angle of the Haut
Arolla gl.   More complicated on the seldom visited Ital. side
(S and E).   An object of disparaging remarks in Alpine literature, largely redeemed today. The unadopted name of Pte.
Marcel Kurz is used by the Italians to identify the large snow
dome pt. 3498.3m. situated halfway along the W ridge from
Col Collon. First ascent: A. Cust with a guide he refused to
name, 7 August, 1876.

West Ridge (from Col Collon). A good snow rte. but liable to
form bad cornices in some seasons.   F+.   First recorded
ascent, but probably not the first, in 1892.

56 From the Col Collon hut follow Rte. 5 to the hollow under
(S of) La Vierge, immediately before the col and just N of
pt. 3098m. (1 h.).   From the Bouquetins biv. hut reverse
Rte. 5 to Col Collon (1 h.) and move L (SE) into the hollow.
Climb scree and snow to a continuous and fairly steep snow/ice
slope rising to an apex due E. Well below this trend R to join

the ridge at a snow/rubble shoulder, pt. 3283.1m. Continue up the snow ridge, narrowing, possibly corniced and delicate, over the apex and finally reaching pt. 3498.3m. In good snow conditions it is equally possible to climb the apex direct without moving R to the lower ridge. Now descend the snow crest into saddle pt. 3424m., then climb the summit snow crest, probably corniced, in a nice position above the N face to the top ($1\frac{1}{2}$-2 h., $2\frac{1}{2}$-3 h. from either hut).

North-East Ridge (from Col de Tsa de Tsan). Until recent times the most frequented way up the mtn. Loose unpleasant rock on the ridge, otherwise not difficult. PD-. First ascensionists.

57 From the Bouquetins biv. hut cross the gl. plateau SE with some crevasses into the corner below the Col de Tsa de Tsan (3243m.) which above a small bergschrund is reached by a broad snow slope ($1\frac{1}{4}$ h.). From the col climb the straightforward and fairly steep rock ridge, very rotten in places, turning short steps on the L, to cross a cairned forepeak (3538m.) where a short sharp snow crest leads to the top ($1\frac{1}{2}$ h., $2\frac{3}{4}$ h. from hut).

North Face. A fairly short but serious mixed climb, harder in summer than in good winter conditions. Early summer conditions with good snow on the lower slabs are essential for safety. The overhanging bergschrund needs a lot of good snow, even to get across with considerable difficulty, while the upper rocks must be mainly snow free. Minimal stonefall. 400m. D+/TD. Ranked by the British party as harder than the Cheilon N face. First ascent: M. Brandt, J. Braun, A. Meyer, R. Theytaz, M. Zuckschwerdt, 27 June, 1965. In winter: J. R. Affolter, R. Monnerat, 4 January, 1975. First British ascent: L. N. Griffin, C. Torrans, early July, 1975. Solo: D. Heymans, 15 August, 1974.

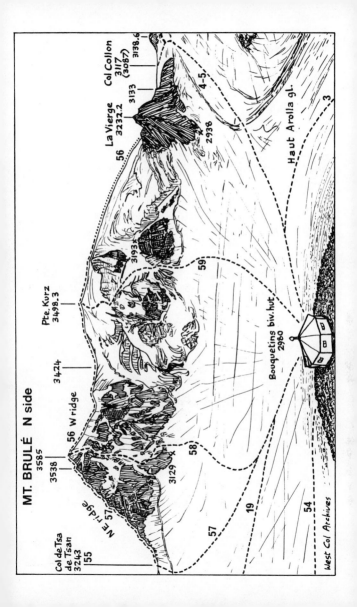

MT. BRULÉ N side

Col de Tsa de Tsan 3243
55

NE ridge
57

3585
3538

56 W ridge

3424

Pte. Kurz 3498.3

3193×

La Vierge 3232.2

56

Col Collon 3117 (3087)
3138.6

3133

×2938

4–5

3

Haut Arolla gl.

3129×

58

59

57

19

Bouquetins biv. hut 2980

54

West Col Archives

58 From the Bouquetins biv. hut approach over the almost flat gl. plain to the foot of the face in 1 h. or less. Cross the bergschrund to the R of a slabby spur (3129m.) and ascend steep snow/ice for a rope length to where a rising traverse L over slabs leads up steeply to the spur crest line. This section can be difficult and delicate if the slabs are not covered with snow or ice. Now ascend direct via three rock islets to the steep central snow/ice field (54°) which is climbed on the R. Reach the upper rocks and take these direct with pitches of III, IV. Slant R and emerge on the summit snowcap (4 h. from bergschrund).

59 <u>North Spur of Pt. 3498.3m.</u> An interesting ice climb with some danger from sérac fall. Starts up the broken ice face just L of rock buttress pt. 3193m. and meanders up bearing L to reach an easier final slope. 400m. D/D+ (4-5 h.). First ascent: U. Manera, G. C. Ricompensa, 10 August, 1962. In winter: M. Dandelot, F. Deshusses, J. Jenny, R. Jossen, 22 December, 1974 (3 h.). Solo: D. Heymans, 15 August, 1974 - same day as N face of main summit.

COL COLLON 3117m.

LK 1347. An old and easy gl. pass, across which cattle used to be driven many years ago, from Arolla to the Valpelline. See Rtes. 4, 5, 20.

Collon - Pigne - Aigs. Rouges Groups

A disparate collection of the best known peaks in the Arolla area, round the S and W sides of the valley from where they are mostly unseen except for the monumental hulk of Mt. Collon.

COL DE L'EVÊQUE 3392m.

LK 1347. Fine gl. pass between the Ptes. d'Oren and L'Evêque, a stage on the High Level Route. See Rte. 4. Crossed by a Swiss surveyor, c. 1835. First recorded tourist traverse: E. N. Buxton, K. E. Digby with F. Biner and two others, 10 August, 1863.

L'EVÊQUE 3716.3m.

LK 1347. A steep and elegant rock and snow peak, a popular excursion from the Vignettes hut. Climbs on the E side are now more attractive following the appearance of the Bouquetins biv. hut. The usual rtes. have been undergraded in the past. First ascent: A. Baltzer, C. Schroeder, 5 August, 1867.

North Flank and North-East Ridge. A pleasant snow climb except in late season when crevasses and the bergschrund can be troublesome. Ice and icy rocks not infrequent on the steep upper ridge flank. PD. First ascensionists.

60 From the Vignettes hut start as for Rte. 4 and cross the Mt. Collon gl. plateau due E to reach the foot of the large gl. slope descending NW between L'Evêque and the Mitre. Climb this slope keeping L, some crevasses, to reach snow saddle 3528m. at the top (2½ h.). Now ascend a fairly steep snow/ice slope on the R (W) side of the NE ridge, above a band of ice cliffs below and further R, to join the ridge at a sloping snow saddle on the L. Ascend trending R below ridge crest line again, cross a bergschrund and continue straight up snow/ice plaques to some rocks on the ridge proper to your L, then up to the summit (1-1½ h., 3½-4 h. from hut).

South-West Ridge (from Col de l'Evêque). A popular climb on sound rock if the crest or slight variations on the R (S) side are followed. The steep step is more easily tackled on the L (W) side but this tends to be icy and the rock is a bit loose. AD-, with short pitches of III and one of IV. First ascent: Miss A.M. Barrett, E.H. & H. Barrett, R.A. Robertson with J. Quinodoz, A. Tembl, 18 August, 1894.

61 From the Vignettes hut follow Rte. 4 to the Col de l'Evêque (3392m.) (2¼ h.). From the Bouquetins hut to the Col de l'Evêque also by Rte. 4 in about the same time.

Above the col follow the ridge line up snow and some easy rocks over a snow dome (3465m.) to a saddle below (3399m.). This saddle can be reached directly from the gl. below on the Vignettes side by a somewhat steeper ascent on snow and normally saves 20 min. Above, turn an initial ridge step somewhat on the L by snowy rocks, then return to the crest and follow it to the foot of a steep step. Move up R to a little gully and climb this (III) to a ledge under a steep wall. Traverse L below bulging rock, then across a cracked slab (IV) to rejoin the crest by a short wall L. Follow the sharp crest (II+) with a few pinnacled obstacles overhanging the S side on excellent rock to the top. Practised alternatives include: From top of little gully take a steep ramp/ledge line R on S side of ridge and rejoin ridge higher up (III+), or from foot of step ascend trending L on steep slabby rock with snow and return up a fine flake crack to the crest at the top of the step (III+) (2 h., 4¼ h. from either hut).

East Ridge. A blunt projection, barely discernible on map on

76

which it resembles a gangway slanting steeply upwards from the foot of an ice couloir directly below the saddle/col 3528m., to near the summit of L'Evêque. Higher up the main feature is a big V gully with the more pronounced ridge on its L. An increasingly frequented rock climb of high quality, recommended. 550m. TD-, pitches of V/V+. First ascent: P. Diethelm, M. Ebneter, 9 August, 1962. In winter, solo: D. Neuenschwander, 12 January, 1976.

62 From the Bouquetins biv. hut ascend the Haut Arolla gl. easily to the foot of the E side of the mtn. (45 min.). Start well to the L of the ice couloir, at a rock toe at c.3140m. Climb straightforward slabs (III) to some small ledges, then a dièdre (IV) above these. From a large block move along a narrow ledge slanting diagonally R (IV), then traverse L (V, peg) and reach the ridge crest. Climb pleasant slabs for 80m. (III, IV), followed by two fine pitches (V) which lead to the foot of a grey buttress. Cross an obvious couloir L and climb the buttress by a wide dièdre (V, 2 pegs). After another rope length, traverse somewhat R over large slabs (III, IV) for about 100m. Reach the foot of a yellow buttress. Traverse R over large slabs to the foot of a small dièdre filled with chockstones. Climb it (IV+) and continue up slabs trending R (20m., III, IV).

Now take a ledge line L (IV, peg), then climb a smooth vertical wall (V+, peg) which leads to some smooth slabby walls. Turn them on the L (IV) and climb another series of slabby walls (90m., III, IV). Approach the final buttress. Start up its L side, slanting in this direction (IV, IV+), and reach a ledge which appears suddenly (peg). On the R, climb an overhang (IV+), then a short vertical step (V), followed by a traverse L across the wall (IV) to where you can climb direct to a good platform (V+, peg). Move R and climb a small conspicuous dièdre (IV, V, V+, exit VI) and reach some smooth loose slabs (V) which form a sort of couloir. From a niche, cross smooth

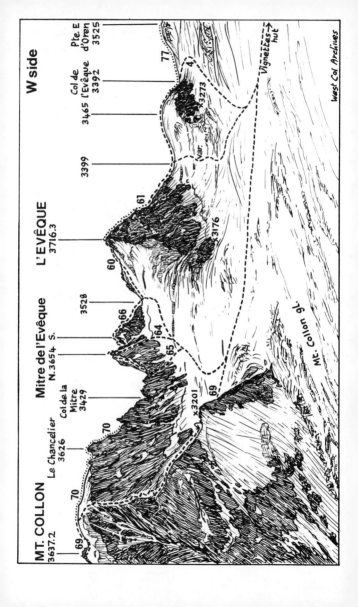

W side

MT. COLLON 3637.2   Le Chancelier 3626   Mitre de l'Evêque N.3654 S.   L'EVÊQUE 3716.3   3399   3465 l'Evêque 3392   Col de l'Evêque   Pte. E d'Oren 3525

Col de la Mitre 3429

3528

Vignettes → hut

Mt. Collon gl.

West Col Archives

slabs (V+) into the big couloir, which is climbed easily for 10m. Then rejoin immediately the crest of the buttress (IV). Continue up the buttress (IV+/V) to the final crest which has a gendarme giving a pitch of V+ ($8\frac{1}{2}$ h. from foot of face).

63 East Face Pillar. See preamble to Rte. 62. The obvious pillar/ridge flanking the R side of the big V gully in the top half of the face, which in turn is bordered L by the E Ridge of Rte. 62. The pillar descends quite prominently into walls immediately above the L side of the ice couloir coming down from near saddle/col 3528m. A direct rte. from the foot of the couloir was pursued up it by Mme. G. Grimm, J. J. Grimm, R. Monnerat, M. Vallat, 7 June, 1976. 500m., several pitches of V and one of V+, 10 h.

MITRE DE L'EVÊQUE 3654m.

LK 1347. Sharp rock peak with large twin prongs, N (highest) and S, giving short, interesting rock climbs. First ascent: A. Cust with P. Beytrison, J. Martin, 22 September, 1879.

West Face. The easiest rte., mixed ground, broken rock, stonefall after midday. PD. Only recommended for ascent. First ascensionists, in descent.

64 From the Vignettes hut follow Rte. 60 to the foot of the face. Start above a broken area of gl. round a steep rock wall/toe, where a snow slope at c. 3440m. rises into a gully just L of the summit line, about where the figures 3654 are printed on map (2 h.). Climb this gully on poor rock and snow/ice bits to mid height, then follow steep shattered rock on its R side to the summit ($1\frac{1}{4}$ h., $3\frac{1}{4}$ h. from hut).

North-North-West Ridge (from Col de la Mitre). The usual rte., popular, quite steep and technical at the top. PD+ with short pitches of III.   First ascensionists.

65 From the Vignettes hut start as for Rte. 60 and trend L to a line directly below the Col de la Mitre (3429m.). A snow couloir divides a fairly broad mass of rock L and a narrow rib R.   Cross a bergschrund, climb snow to the R hand rib and follow this for 50m. to move L halfway up into the couloir; or climb couloir from the bottom; then up the steep couloir to the col/gap (2 h.). Follow the pleasant slabby ridge crest to the steeper upper section. Halfway up the steep part traverse L for a few m. and climb a steep 10m. pitch (III) to rejoin the crest. Or traverse R and climb a rising ledge line with moves of III to rejoin the crest.   Now reach the sharp top in a few min. (2 h., 4 h. from hut).

<u>South-South-West Ridge (over South Summit).</u> An obvious rte., with loose but not difficult rock.   Crossing the gap between the two summits is also loose and steep. PD+ with pitches of III. Easier in reverse direction, by abseiling from the N (main) summit into gap.   First ascent: C.L. & T.G. Longstaff with J. Maître, P. Maurys, 3 August, 1897. Complete traverse to N summit, probably not until 1924, then from N to S.

66 From the Vignettes hut follow Rte. 60 to snow saddle 3528m. ($2\frac{1}{2}$ h.).   Climb the easy but loose ridge to the top of the S summit (30 min.).   Descend the serrated ridge, sometimes with awkward snow knobs (II) into the gap. Above, a wall defends the N summit, in which there are several dièdres. On the L the easiest is the loosest; climb this (III) to the top; abseil in descent (40 min. from S summit, $3\frac{3}{4}$ h. from hut). More frequently done in reverse direction.

67 <u>East Ridge.</u>   At the bottom this ridge flares out NE as a big gully seamed buttress called the Echos de Collon with twin summits (3294m.).   The ridge is reached up a broken rock rib immediately L of a big rock gully L of the inner buttress summit, on the S side of the ridge. Near the top of this rib trend L to a gap at the foot of the ridge proper. Follow the ridge direct on improving rock all the way to top of N summit. Two large gendarmes on the upper part are turned on the R side, the second being the crux. No precise details. Pitches of III+/IV. About 5½ h. from Bouquetins biv. hut. First ascent: G. Arbuthnot, C. Oppenheim with J. Georges, J. Maître, 6 September, 1895.

68 <u>North-East Rib.</u> Projects into the crevassed bay called the Mitre gl. Climbed to the steep wall section where a move R is made to reach the NNW ridge at the foot of its steep upper section, Rte. 65. No details. About AD+. First ascent: probably A. S. Jenkins and guides in 1924.

COL DE LA MITRE   3427m.

LK 1347. Between the Mitre de l'Evêque and Mt. Collon. Marked but not named on map. Several gaps in ridge at this pt., the most northerly being the measured one. On W side, by Rte. 65. E side, above the Mitre gl., dangerous and not recommended. First traverse: A. Cust with P. Beytrison, J. Martin, 20 September, 1879.

MONT COLLON   3637.2m.

LK 1347. Imposing, massive and rotund mtn. which dominates the head of the Arolla valley, comparable as a landmark with the Matterhorn above the Zermatt valley. The resemblance ends there. It is much more a recognisable and memorable profile than a symbol of great mountaineering interest. Before 1945 nearly always climbed by one or two rtes., although its various facets had received many different but rarely repeated ascents long ago. Arthur Cust's dictum persisted as an attitude for 60 years - "Mont Collon is nothing but the braggart buttress of a ridge whose supreme point is L'Evêque." While modern mountaineering antics have left few marks on the mtn., its more serious rtes. have now gained a respectable following as a result of initiatives mostly taken by the Arolla guides, concerned to raise the climbing status of the Arolla district. It must be added that this interest is also due to generally bolder attitudes in the assessment of objective dangers and better techniques developed elsewhere for the safer passage of loose rock and poorly protected steep mixed ground.

First ascent: G. E. Foster with H. Baumann, J. Krönig, 31 July, 1867.

West Ridge. The normal rte., a popular climb of average interest, loose rock. The best and quickest descent rte. from the mtn. PD/PD+. First ascent: A. Cust, F. Gardiner with H. & P. Knubel, 3 August, 1876.

69 From the Vignettes hut start as for Rte. 60 but after the Col de Chermotane cross the gl. due W (crevasses) to a snow slope on S side of ridge, under a wide snow saddle just R (E) of buttress pt. 3201m. ($1\frac{1}{4}$ h.). Ascend to this saddle and follow the ridge above by the crest or just R of it, to a big step. Traverse R along a ledge (cairn), descend 2m. and move further R, then ascend easy but very loose rocks and gravel covered ledges to rejoin the crest above the top of the step. Follow the sharp ridge with one pitch of II to the summit snow dome. Cross snow due E to reach the rock tip forming the highest pt. overlooking the Haut Arolla gl. (2 h., $3\frac{1}{4}$ h. from hut).

South-East Flank and South Ridge. The original Arolla rte., now the normal rte. from the Bouquetins hut. Fairly complicated rte. finding; a descent description is also given. Loose rock and gravel littered ledges. PD/PD+. First ascensionists.

70 From the Bouquetins biv. hut cross the Haut Arolla gl. to the big moraine on the other side, near pt. 2878m. Get over this moraine, somewhat disagreeable, and descend the inner side to continue on bad ground towards pt. 2897m. Just before this pt. go up a moraine on the R of a rognon, merging into snow at the R (N) side of the Mitre gl. Follow up this side with some crevasses to the rock headwall at the top (2 h.).

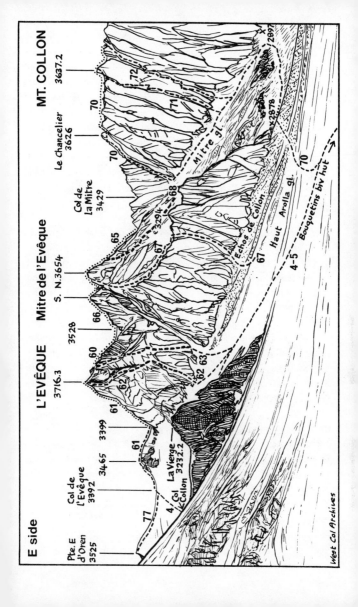

E side

L'ÉVÊQUE   Mitre de l'Evêque   MT. COLLON

Pte. E
d'Oren
3525

Col de
l'Evêque
3392

3465 3399 3716.3   3528   S. N.3654   Col de
                                           la Mitre
                                           3429   Le Chancelier   3637.2
                                                   3626

La Vierge 3232.2

4. Col
   Collon

77

61 61 62 62 60 66 65 67 68 70 70 70 72

63 62

e 329k

Echos de Collon

67 67

Haut Arolla gl.   Mitre gl.

4-5

70

Bouquetins biv hut →

x 2878

x 2897

West Col Archives

Directly above is the Col de la Mitre (3429m.) with an obvious access couloir. Another couloir to the R slants R to the S ridge of the mtn. about halfway up, just behind a large pointed gendarme on the ridge. Cross a bergschrund and follow the generally snowy couloir to its ridge gap. Continue on the crest with poor rock, with ledges and rib traverses as alternatives below on the R (E) side, up to better rock leading steeply to the big gendarme called the Chancelier (3626m.). This can be traversed (III) but it is better to turn it low down on the R side along a ledge system, to reach the gap behind. Ascend from the gap by a short chimney and broken rocks to the summit snowfield. Trend NE over a snowcap to the highest pt. (2 h., 4 h. from biv. hut).

In descent: Follow snow to the edge of the drop into the gap in front of the Chancelier gendarme. Descend a short chimney to the gap. Do not ascend the gendarme. Instead, traverse L on the E side along a horizontal line and rejoin S ridge at foot of the steep riser under the Chancelier. Now descend S ridge, quickest by zigzags on its E flank, following small rock ribs (cairns) to the upper edge of big walls overlooking the Mitre gl. (large cairn). From here traverse R (S) along an easy ledge leading towards the large snow couloir coming down from a gap behind a large pointed gendarme situated halfway up the S ridge. Descend the snow couloir to a bergschrund at the bottom; Mitre gl. ($1\frac{1}{2}$ h. in descent to this pt.).

South-East (Sunrise) Pillar. The narrow pillar falling directly from the summit pt. to the Mitre gl. at c.3120m. Approach from Bouquetins biv. hut by Rte. 70 in $1\frac{1}{4}$ h. Rock good except for 2 pitches in middle part and at the top where climbing is easy. 520m., 20 pitches, D, pitches of IV+ and one of V. All pegs removed on first ascent: J. B. Fellay, J. Jenny, C. Pisteur, 13 July, 1975.

71 Climb the edge of the pillar for 5 pitches (II, III, IV), then move L from a large rock finger up partly overhanging rock, a delicate wall (IV+, peg) and dièdre, to a stance in a little dièdre. Take another dièdre to rejoin the crest and go up this by a detached flake (IV+). Continue on slabs (IV) to the foot of a big red gendarme which is turned on the L. Climb a dièdre (III) to rejoin crest where slabs lead for 2 pitches on the edge (IV+). Turn a 30m. tower on the L, up a chimney, and rejoin crest. A wall/tower rises above. Climb the R side of wall for 5m., traverse 5m. horizontally L, climb 3m., then traverse diagonally R to reach a shoulder (V, delicate, 3 pegs). Work up R side of shoulder along a broken ramp, cross a stony gully then ascend diagonally R over loose rock to finish this section at a shoulder. Above, climb two vertical steps of red rock by dièdre/chimneys to belay among blocks (IV+, 2 pegs). Continue for 10m. on R of crest by an easy ramp, then take a steep pitch (III) for 7m. to a belay. Now climb a crack for 5m., then traverse 20m. L (peg, delicate) to exit up a crack on to a shoulder. From here climb steep, loose easy rock to the summit ($7\frac{1}{2}$ h. from foot of pillar).

72 <u>South-East (Towers Route) Pillar</u>. Situated immediately R of the Sunrise Pillar, Rte. 71, identical approach. Generally good rock throughout, 500m., D, pitches of IV+/V. First ascent: M. Barthassat, J. L. Nicolas, 13 July, 1975 (same day as Sunrise Pillar).

<u>North Face</u>

This broad, semi-circular face - Foster's "decapitated Matter-horn" - looks down on Arolla. Visible from the valley, the L profile marks the NNE ridge, the R the W ridge. An "E ridge" lies behind the NNE one on the generally very loose E flank of the mtn. below pt. 3563m.
    Between the limits described are three equidistant and more or less poorly defined ridges which account for the main rtes., although most of the secondary features between them have also been climbed. The NNE ridge at the L side is quite a good climb; the L or E-central buttress on the face gives the

Hopkinson Rte., the R or W-central buttress the Gracey Rte., both being serious mixed climbs; midway between the Gracey buttress and the W ridge is a vaguely defined NW ridge called the Schwartz Rte., which has little to commend it.

73 <u>North-North-East Ridge.</u> Poorly indicated on LK25, better on LK50. Descends from pt. 3563m. over pt. 3284m. The foot of the ridge is broad, vague and normally started from the Haut Arolla gl. at 2700m. by traversing a scree terrace NW above a rockband, soon returning L to mount slabby, rounded L flank for 300m. to where the crest is evident. All this section is steep but can be climbed within grade II. A little higher the ridge narrows, forming a series of pinnacles, the first being pt. 3284m. Some of them are traversed, others turned R along snowbands, others L on fairly easy rock. A steep step climbed direct on good holds (III) leads to the vague junction with a NE branch of the ridge; this branch was descended by R. C. Gilson with P. Maître and a porter, 12 August, 1890 - easier than the corresponding section on the NNE ridge proper. The final ridge consists of several small teeth and gaps, concluded with a headwall. PD+/AD, 4 h. from gl. in good conditions. First ascent: W. W. Naismith with J. Quinodoz, 15 August, 1895. In winter: P. G. Combaz, J. Rey, 7 January, 1978.

<u>Left Central Ridge (Hopkinson Route).</u> A huge lower buttress supports the upper part of the ridge and the R edge of the buttress defines the most obvious line. This edge is divided from an even larger buttress further R (Gracey Rte.) by a big central couloir. The rock toe below the R side of this couloir is pt. 2474m. A long mixed climb on fair to good rock with variable technical ice problems at the top. The first section up to and across the central couloir is exposed to stonefall which may be bad in poor conditions. Normally easier than the Gracey Rte. 1100m., D-/D. First ascent: J. Hopkinson

with A. & J. Maître, 13 August, 1890. In winter: L. Favre, Candide Pralong, 1 February, 1969 (8½ h.).

74 Approach from the Arolla valley roadhead up the Bas Arolla gl. tongue without difficulty in 1½ h. to foot of face, pt. 2474m. Work round and R of rock toe, away from the large avalanche debris cone below the central couloir, then go up snow (bergschrund) and a few rocks to a narrow snowband along foot of face proper. Traverse L below initial rockband cut by little gullies to where, directly above pt. 2474m. a little inlet gives access to a short ramp slanting R to reach top of the initial rockband. This pt. can also be reached more directly up the R side of the avalanche cone (potentially more exposed to stonefall), i.e. up the L side of rock toe, then moving R to enter the inlet/ramp.

Above, a huge gangway feature rises steeply L, narrowing higher up. Climb it on snow and rock, in the middle part following a slight rib R or rocks below it L, up to where two apparent ledge line exits appear. Take the lower one in a rising traverse above the central gully to emerge at the lower end of a snow/rock bowl where the gully opens out. Cross the gully L, fairly easy at this pt. (stonefall) and climb steep mixed ground, trending L to near the rounded edge of the buttress which is followed directly to the prominent black shoulder at the top (2-2½ h.).

Continue along a fairly straightforward rock ridge with minor obstacles to a drop above an awkward snow filled gap. Descend rocks on the L (E) side before the gap and pass along the hanging gl. on this side, to reascend to the ridge immediately after the gap. The continuation ridge is uniformly steep in four unequal steps divided by snow/ice parts, normally delicate and sustained with several pitches of III. Finally reach a sharp ice crest which mounts for 75m. into the upper L end of the narrow, necklace-like sérac band hanging below the summit snowfield (2½-4 h.). Original exit. Leave the ridge just before the ice

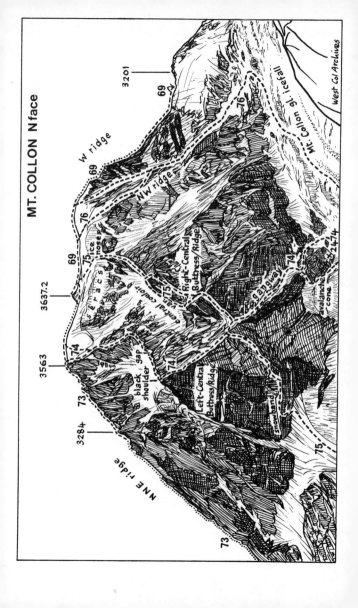

MT. COLLON N face

3201
69
W ridge
69
NW ridge
76
69
ice nose
75
séracs
central couloir
75
Right-Central Buttress/Ridge
74
gangway
74
74
avalanche cone
12-74
Left-Central Buttress/Ridge
74
snow mound
75
3637.2
3563
74
74
black shoulder gap
73
106
3284
73
NNE ridge

Mt. Collon gl. icefall
West Col Archives

crest and ascend diagonally R on steep snow/ice to breach the
sérac band at a low pt., invariably with 15-20m. of hard ice
work.   Then directly above by a steep snow/ice slope, soon
easing off but with a long crevasse guarding the exit, turned
on R to reach the snowcap well R of pt. 3563m.   In favourable
conditions the ice crest can be climbed to exit at the upper L
end of the sérac band, generally steeper and harder, finishing
just R of pt. 3563m.   The most sensible exit is to follow the
ice crest for one pitch, then traverse L off it for another pitch
to reach a steep rock rib, often icy, leading directly to
pt. 3563m. (pitches of III+/IV) (2-2$\frac{1}{2}$ h., 6$\frac{1}{2}$-9 h. from foot of
face).

Right Central Ridge (Gracey Route).   A serious mixed climb
of considerable character and interest, still climbed infrequently because good conditions for the exit are rare.   The
climb is reasonably free from stonefall; both this and the lower
rock difficulties can be reduced by starting up the Hopkinson
Rte.   Common practice.   At the top, the crux is an ice nose
formation similar to but generally harder than the Mönch Nollen
and Scerscen Eisnase.   1000m., D+ with pitches of IV.   First
ascent: Miss L. Gracey with M. Pralong father & son, 20
July, 1923 (14$\frac{1}{2}$ h.).   In winter: Cyrille Pralong, M. Siegenthaler, 1 February, 1969 (11$\frac{1}{4}$ h.).

75 Original start.   Approach from the Arolla valley roadhead,
taking the lower path up the L (E) side of the Bas Arolla gl.
via pt. 2370m.   Go into the zigzags near pt. 2496m. where the
main gl. torrent must be crossed.   As this might be difficult
it may be better to join the surface of the gl. before pt. 2370m.
and go up the ice and rubble into the narrows near pt. 2496m.
Now ascend a snow slope almost due S of this pt., which broadens up to the foot of the face.   Keep R and cross a moraine
bank to reach the foot of the large black buttress which supports
the Hopkinson Rte.   The buttress is reached to the L (E) of its

L hand corner, at its NE facet. Here a line of weakness extends diagonally R, going round the edge on to the NW side of the buttress ($2\frac{1}{2}$ h.).

Follow the weakness R, easy at the start with a snowband and rocks to a steep chimney (IV) leading on to the buttress corner. Continue across a large shallow slabby depression (III), going along a snowy ledge round another corner to reach the R (W) edge of the buttress above the central couloir. Descend and cross the couloir (stonefall), then climb a buttress directly above to a snow/scree shoulder, at the foot of the upper part of the right central buttress. Follow its steep slabby crest with a pillar/step halfway up, usually turned L up a series of chimneys (III/IV). The upper crest is generally snowy and levels out before a final steep icy rock rib under the sérac wall supporting the summit snowfield. Two short vertical rock pitches, the slabby rib and the wall climbed by an ice nose or by the most feasible weakness that can be found, at least 40m. before the plain slope above can be reached (12-15 h. from foot of face). The second ascensionists followed the Hopkinson Rte. to the central couloir crossing pt. , and thus avoided the gully crossing itself. Quicker and safer. Mme. A. Hermann with P. Maurys, H. Trovaz in 1937.

76 <u>North-West Ridge.</u> Divided from the upper Gracey ridge by an enormous shallow snow/ice couloir. Below that the rocks are nearly merged together in a series of thin parallel ribs. The lower part of the ribbed face is turned, not easily, on the R and the main ridge rib is joined higher up. At mid height a break in the steepness before the final mixed rib and a very difficult ice wall exit. On the R of this section is the NW face couloir. Altogether, steep, loose, mixed ground with considerable stonefall danger. Not recommended. 850m. , D+. First ascent: M. Schwartz with J. Georges de Martin, J. Georges le Skieur, 23 July, 1921. In winter (solo): A. Georges,

25-26 February, 1974. NW couloir: M. Dandelot, J. B. Fellay, J. Jenny, 23 February, 1975 (8 h. from foot of face).

POINTES D'OREN   E. 3525m.   C. 3487m.   W. 3490.1m.

77 LK 1347. Ital: Becca d'Oren. The frontier ridge between the Col de l'Evêque and Col d'Oren, easily reached from the former by a gentle snow slope, but with some loose rock climbing up the ridge from latter col. Rarely visited. Traversed by E. Canzio, F. Mondini, N. Vigna with G. Noro, 26 August, 1897.

COL DU PETIT MONT COLLON   3292m.

LK 1347.   Gl. saddle between Petit Mt. Collon and the Pte. d'Oren Central.   Part of the High Level Route between the Otemma gl. and Col de l'Evêque.   Large crevasses hereabouts in late summer, the best crossing place is 200m. S of the lowest pt.

PETIT MONT COLLON   E. 3555.5m.   W. 3538m.

LK 1346, 1347.   A curiously isolated and fine rock and snow elevation adjoining the Col de Chermotane, from the Vignettes hut assailed by all-comers. It has only become popular in the last 30 years. First ascent: probably W. B. Rickman with J. Ansevui, J. Vuigner, 1872.

<u>South Side of West Summit</u>. The easiest rte., F+/PD-. Descended by W. Larden, D. Wyatt-Smith with J. Maître, 1 September, 1905.

78 Reach the SW base of the mtn. on the Otemma gl. from the Vignettes hut or Chanrion hut by Rte. 7 (1¼ h. or 4 h.). About 400m. distance N of pt. 3000m., climb the alternate snow/rock band near its R end, up a steep snowy opening to the crevassed gl. slopes running up NE to below the S side of the mtn., this side being only 150m. high (45 min.). A slight depression rises to the lowest ridge col close to the W summit further L. On the R climb a steep loose rock rib to the col/gap, then follow the main ridge E on rock and snow over an intermediate rock top to a snow crest and the E summit (1¼ h., 3¼ h. from Vignettes hut, 6 h. from Chanrion hut).

Further R, the SW facet of the E summit can be climbed direct on steep broken rock with a loose chimney, PD. Descended by W.H. Gover, J.W. Wyatt with P.A. Perren, 16 August, 1904.

79 North-West Ridge of West Summit. An obvious and direct rte. from the Vignettes hut. Loose rock. AD/AD+. At pt. 3106m. (45 min.) turn the first part of the ridge above the Col de Chermotane by climbing L up the steep icy edge of the N face to join the crest above the initial step at a level snow bit, about 125m. above the height of the bergschrund across the N face. Continue up the mixed crest to a step which is best climbed direct, followed by a fine snow crest to W summit (about 4 h. from foot of ridge). J. & B. Hopkinson with A. & J. Maître, 18 August, 1890.

North Face of West Summit. A triangular snow/ice face immediately seen from the Vignettes hut. Short and now popular, a good technical exercise in ice climbing, though good snow throughout can be found in early season, no objective danger, 45 min. walk from hut. 350m., 55° average angle with steeper bits, D-/D. First ascent: probably A. Bernard, R. Tissières, June, 1940. In winter: M. Brandt, J. Braun, 1 March, 1965. Solo: D. Heymans, 10 July, 1972. Descended on ski by A. Anzevui, C. Genolet, 9 April, 1974.

80 Directly below the W summit climb steep snow to the bergschrund, cross this and continue up the fluted snow/ice face straight to the top (3 h. on average).

PETIT MT. COLLON
N Face

E 3555.5   W 3538

78

81   80   79

3106

Col de Chermotane

81 <u>North-North-East Face of East Summit</u>. A pleasant climb, above the bergschrund a snow/ice slope for the first third, then steep snowy rocks with a delicate iceband near the top. The line taken is absolutely direct, 350m., D-. First ascent: M. Brandt, R. Theytaz, R. Voillat, 3 August, 1961. British ascent: G. Hardie, J. Higham, 1972.

COL DE CHERMOTANE   3053m.

LK 1346, 1347. Huge gl. saddle at top of the Otemma gl., crossed by several important approaches between the Vignettes, Chanrion and Bouquetins huts. See Rtes. 4, 7. First tourist crossing: E. N. & T. F. Buxton, J. J. Cowell with M. Payot, 16 August, 1861.

PIGNE D'AROLLA   3796m.

LK 1346, 1347. For Arolla attractive as an outstanding view-point as the Breithorn is for Zermatt. The Mediterranean can be seen from the summit. A planning application to build a cableway to the summit was defeated in the early 1960s. A snow peak with plenty to commend it and popular for a traverse back to Arolla. First ascent: A. W. Moore, H. Walker with J. Anderegg, 9 July, 1865.

<u>East-South-East Flank</u>. The normal rte., all on snow, trail in mid-season. F/F+. The more direct approach through the icefall above the hut is seldom possible without some effort and loss of time. First ascent: J.H. Isler with J. Gillioz, 24 August, 1866.

82 From the Vignettes hut cross the Col des Vignettes, then traverse S along a snow terrace under the E icefall spur of the mtn. Descend SSW over a scree/rock barrier towards the Col de Chermotane, then traverse round below the barrier and ascend NW by a wide and fairly steep icy couloir, with pt. 3189.4m. further L. Bear up WNW over easy angled but very crevassed snow slopes to the saddle on S side of summit, or trend more to N, keeping close to E ridge - latter is steeper but less crevassed. From the saddle ascend easy snow to the top. Variable, according to disposition of crevasses from year to year (2 h. from hut).

West Flank (by Col du Brenay). The normal rte. from the Dix hut, again all on snow and crevassed glaciers. Done in the reverse direction, one of the most popular expeditions from the Vignettes hut for traversing the mtn., back to Arolla. Route finding problems in poor visability. F/F+. First ascensionists.

83 From the Dix hut descend to the Cheilon gl. Cross its moraines and ice SE to the gl. branch of Tsena Réfien. Go up the L (N) wing of this gl., L of the dividing rock barrier pt. 3029m., keeping L under the Tsena Réfien rocks. The slopes are usually badly crevassed. Above the level of the dividing barrier trend S and SW on to a large gl. spur rising towards the Col de la Serpentine. Follow this with some large crevasses, easily avoided, for half the distance to the latter col, to c. 3500m. Now contour slopes to your L (SE) and climb a steep snow slope some distance SW of pt. 3592m., which leads without incident but with more crevasses round a shoulder to the plateau depression of the Col du Brenay (3639m.) ($2\frac{1}{2}$ - 3 h.). From here climb gentle snow slopes NE to the summit (30 min., 3-$3\frac{1}{2}$ h. from Dix hut; $1\frac{1}{2}$-2 h. in descent). Return across the Pas de Chèvres by Rte. 10 to reach Arolla.

North Face. Over several decades this climb has gradually become the most classic snow/ice and mixed rte. of its class in the Arolla district. The face itself is only 300m. at an angle of 50° above its bergschrund but there is varied and interesting work below this. The rock is generally loose but does not exceed II+. The upper half of the face is sometimes a sheet

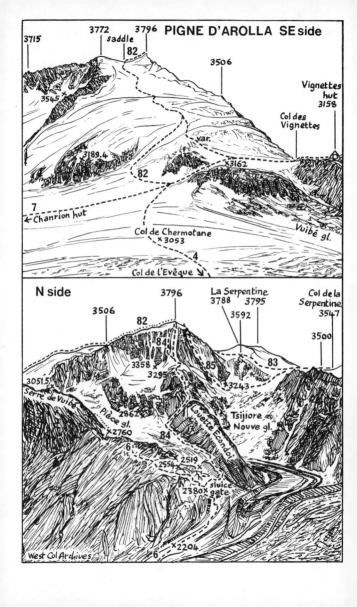

PIGNE D'AROLLA SE side

3715

3772
saddle

3796

82

3506

Vignettes hut
3158

3545

Col des Vignettes

×3189.4

82

×3162

var.

7

← Chanrion hut

Vuibé gl.

Col de Chermotane
×3053

4

Col de l'Evêque ↓

N side

3506

3796

La Serpentine
3788 3795

Col de la Serpentine
3547

82

84

3592

85

83

3500

3358

3295

3051.5

×3243

Serre de Vuibe

2862

Pièce gl.

Tsijiore
Nouve gl.

×2760

84

2554

2519
×

6

2380×

sluice
gate

West Col Archives

×2204

6

of black ice, and in these conditions the Gardner rib variation can be used. The situations are fine and there is almost no objective danger. Easier than the Argentière N face and Liskamm NE face Neruda rte. AD+/D, according to conditions.

First ascent: A. G. Topham with J. Maître, 5 August, 1889. Rib variation descended by Miss C. M. Gardner with two guides, 13 September, 1889. In ascent: probably G. L. Collins, G. A. Solly, J. M. A. Thomson, 7 August, 1911. In winter: R. Matthey, A. Meyer, 28 February, 1965. Winter solo: A. Georges, 30-31 January, 1973. Descended on ski by A. Anzevui, C. Genolet, 3 April, 1974. Gardner rib var. in winter: R. Monnerat, M. Vallat, 22 March, 1978. Rpt. Anstruther, 1978.

84 From Arolla follow Rte. 6 to the sluice gate at top of moraine (signpost). Ignore usual way L to Vignettes hut and take a track R, in a moraine trench due S to follow up the rubble and ice slopes on R (W) side of the Pièce gl. Go up to 2850m., small inlet on map. On the R, the Louette Econdoi ridge is cut by an obvious scree/snow gully. Ascend this over old avalanche debris, snow and rocks quite steeply to the ridge gap at the top (3 h.). Follow the broad ridge S up steep broken rock to a small snow/ice slope about two rope lengths long, then more rocks and a snow crest lead to a little plateau and snow shoulder pt. 3295m. (1 h.). Take a sharp but easy angled snow crest curving R, returning L to reach a large snowcap. This section can sometimes be done more conveniently on L side of crest. Now below the face go up a steepening snow slope to the bergschrund, fairly large and normally best crossed somewhat L of centre (45 min.). Conditions permitting, ascend the plain snow/ice face directly in the summit line to rocks about 80m. below the top. Either ascend these, or take an icy gutter R, and exit at the snowcap, possibly with a small cornice (3-4 h., $7\frac{3}{4}$-$8\frac{3}{4}$ h. from Arolla).

Left hand (Gardner) Rib. This can be taken when the face is very icy. Cross the bergschrund and make a steep rising traverse L on snow/ice to the low relief rib. Move up to its blunt crest where the rock is soundest; very friable on the flanks. Climb the steep vague crest line on broken rock to a nearly level little shoulder about halfway up. Continue on the steeper top section up to a short, elongated rockband supporting the summit snowcap on its L side. Traverse R on snow and rock to where the cornice above relents, then climb half R on to snowcap (normally 1 h. shorter than climbing middle of face).

Note: Parties starting from the Vignettes hut can descend to the foot of the gully above the Pièce gl. at 2850m. in 45 min., and can therefore accomplish the rte. in approx. $6\frac{1}{2}$ h. from this hut.

85 <u>North-West Face</u>. Described as a fine mixed climb with sound rock and little objective danger, comparable with but more sure than the Cheilon N face. Follows a narrow gully depression immediately L of pronounced rib marking L side of face, in summit line. Initially hard ice pitches then easier work on snow/ice and rock, with a delicate traverse L over a snowband near the top. 500m., TD-. The best approach is from the Dix hut by Rte. 83, over the shoulder of the Col de Tsijiore Nouve, then down crevassed gl. slopes to E for 200m. ($2\frac{1}{2}$ h.). First ascent: B. Agustoni, M. Dandelot, B. Pivot, 19 July, 1972 ($11\frac{1}{2}$ h. from foot of face).

PAS DE CHÈVRES 2855m.

LK 1346. Between Arolla and the Dix hut, large waymarked trail. See Rte. 10. Some 200m. further N is the Col de Ried-matten (2919m.) with an overgrown trail where it diverges from the Pas de Chèvres one, but formerly used frequently. The ridge between the Pas de Chèvres and Col de Tsena Réfien (2952m.) gives an excellent short rock climb over the Pte. du Pas de Chèvres (2991m.) with several gendarmes and good rock (III).

AIGUILLES ROUGES D'AROLLA   3646m.

LK 1326. Superb saw tooth ridge nearly 2 km. long, flanking W side of the Arolla valley. It has three main summits, described simply as: N Peak (3593.6m.), Central Peak (3646m.), and S Peak (3584m.). An outlying far S peak is marked 3486m. Much of the nomenclature used by climbers for features on the mtn. and accepted by the Swiss does not appear on the map. On excellent granite, the main ridge traverse is the most sought after rock climb in the Arolla district, and is one of the best rtes. of its type in the Alps. The climbing is superior to and aesthetically more satisfying than anything found on the Gds. Dents, and the rock is better (perfect almost everywhere) than that of the Bouquetins and Singla ridges. However, the Aigs. Rouges have neither the altitude nor the ultimate seriousness of remote surroundings possessed by the latter. The Dix (W) side of the ridge is hardly ever climbed. The summits are described individually from N to S.

First ascents: Central and N Peaks: J.H. Isler with J. Gillioz, 23 June, 1870. S Peak: A. Macnamara, W.C. Slingsby, H.W. Topham with J. Maître, 3 September, 1887.

NORTH PEAK   3593.6m.

South Ridge (from North Col). There is an obvious but not especially large gap between the Central and N Peaks, called North Col (c. 3535m.). It provides the normal way to the main ridge, and with the short S ridge above it, the most entertaining rte. to the top of the N Peak. PD with short pitches of II/II+. First ascensionists, in descent.

86 From the Aigs. Rouges hut take a track NW, close to two small tarns, then swing round W and SSW, crossing rocks and moraine, passing just below and E of tarn 2881m., then crossing an outfall and going round the E and S sides of moraine pt. 2926m., to reach the Upper Aigs. Rouges gl. at c.3000m. This detour is now necessary owing to the lower edge of the gl. being precipitous and icy. Ascend the gl. keeping L, under the SE spur of the Central Peak, and arrive below the couloir descending from North Col, between the N Peak (R) and the first gendarme on ridge of the Central Peak (L). This is the R-hand of two couloirs. Cross a normally easy bergschrund and climb steep snow/ice for two pitches to the rocks immediately R of couloir. (In early season, with plenty of good snow, it is quicker to follow the couloir bed all the way). On R side of couloir go up steep slabby rocks broken by ledges, moves of II+, with belays at long intervals, and finally move into couloir some 10-15m. below the top (2 h.). From North Col climb the fine ridge direct on sound rock with short bits of II to summit (30 min., $2\frac{1}{2}$ h. from hut).

87 <u>North-East Face</u>. Adjoining the couloir of Rte. 86, start R of rock toe and climb steep open slabs on sound rock with few belays, directly to summit. III ($1\frac{3}{4}$ h.). W. P. Haskett-Smith, J. M. A. Thomson, 11 August, 1911.

88 <u>North Ridge</u>. Rises from a little col immediately N of the N Peak, with a triangular pinnacle further N. Neither feature indicated on map. From the Upper Aigs. Rouges gl., Rte. 86, climb a large snow wedge to col, then go up ridge keeping somewhat L of crest on loose rock, II-. First ascensionists (3 h. from hut).

CENTRAL PEAK 3646m.

<u>North Ridge (from North Col)</u>. About 150m. of excellent climbing on perfect rock. III. First ascensionists.

89 From the Aigs. Rouges hut to North Col by Rte. 86 (2 h.). Climb the first gendarme by its steep sharp crest and descend to a gap. The ridge above rises in a series of short, near vertical steps. This can be climbed direct with short movements L at grade IV. The normal way is to move R (W) into a small gully emanating from the summit and descending to peter out near the gap. Climb either in its bed, possibly icy, or up slabs on its L side, to about three-quarters height. Now move L, cross the ridge crest and traverse 6m. (not more) on the

E side by a somewhat sensational friction traverse under a large loose-looking block. Then climb direct to join the crest which is followed to the top ($1\frac{1}{2}$ h., $3\frac{1}{2}$ h. from hut).

East Flank. The original rte. on this flank is exposed to stone-fall and the rte. described is mostly free from this danger. Climbed quite frequently, and the most direct way up the Central Peak when departing directly from Arolla. Mixed climbing with steep sound rock at the top. PD+, pitches of III. First ascent: R. H. Hope, W. T. Kirkpatrick, 25 August, 1900.

90 From the Aigs. Rouges hut start as for Rte. 86. When below the moraine shoulder pt. 2926m., make a slightly des-cending traverse SW to the inner (N) end of shoulder pt. 2894m., below the foot of the SE spur of the Central Peak. Now traverse W on moraine under this spur to the N side of the Lower Aigs. Rouges gl. (1 h.). Coming from Arolla, reach this pt. by following the hut path Rte. 8 to pt. 2706m. Leave the path and ascend comfortable moraines due W to the lower end of the gl., then keep R along its NE edge to join the approach from the hut (3 h.).

Ahead, at the top of the gl., a big couloir slants N, called North Couloir, under the E face of the mtn. In good snow conditions and crampons this gives a rapid way up to the shoul-der where the SE spur abuts the E flank. However this couloir is often sprayed by stones and in any case is very steep at the top. The usual way is to mount scree, rocks and snow patches due N, about 200m. R of the couloir, and by trending R reach the SE spur about halfway up. Follow its broken crest to an awkward slab, often snowy, running across the head of North Couloir. Cross this, preferably near the top, and reach the inner end of the shoulder where the SE spur fades into the E facet. Now follow an obvious ledge line L (snow) for 10m., returning sharp R up a ramp overhung by rocks below the S ridge of the mtn. This develops into a chimney, passing under the summit line and continuing towards the N ridge of the mtn. After a pitch in the chimney, and directly below the summit, leave the chimney and make an exposed traverse diagonally L into another chimney which is climbed to a final wall and the top ($3\frac{1}{2}$ h., $4\frac{1}{2}$ h. from hut, $6\frac{1}{2}$ h. from Arolla).

<u>South Ridge (from South Col).</u> South Col (c. 3455m.), the prominent depression in the main ridge between the S and Central Peaks, can be reached directly from below by a somewhat dangerous and difficult climb on the E face. Not recommended. The ridge itself is a section of the main ridge traverse, this part being quite delightful, on solid rock and fairly easy. Pitches of II. A. Tschumi with J. Quinodoz, 24 July, 1885.

91 From the South Col keep generally below crest on R (E) side all the way to the top, along rising ledges and short steps, often snowy, to finish up a short chimney. By the crest direct, bits of III (30 min.).

SOUTH PEAK 3584m.

<u>East Flank and South-West Ridge.</u> The usual way up this peak, which is the finest summit of the Aigs. Rouges. A certain amount of mixed climbing and choice of rte. PD+, pitches of III-. First ascensionists.

92 From the Aigs. Rouges hut follow Rtes. 86, 90 to the Lower Aigs. Rouges gl., and at 2900m. cross the gl. to below an obvious gully coming down from a ridge gap above a horizontal snowband near top of face ($1\frac{1}{2}$ h., or from Arolla direct, 3 h.). The broad couloir entrance is blocked by three little buttresses. Climb steep snow or rubble in the minor gullies at extreme L or R, according to conditions, or by waterworn rocks in the gutter and its flanks between the 1st and 2nd buttresses, counting from the L. Continue up the snow or rubble slope above. At the apex, a narrow rock gully rises to a small saddle R of pt. 3486m. Ignore this. About 50m. lower down on the R, another gully slants steeply R to the L edge of the horizontal snowband. Go up smooth terraced rocks on its L side to snow at the top. Alternatively, about one third way up the gully, cross it R and climb steeply on to a broad rock rib which is followed pleasantly to same place. Now either: Continue up the snowband to a short gully giving access to the ridge gap, called Col Slingsby ($1\frac{1}{4}$ h.), then go up the nice ridge, traversing all the gendarmes without special difficulty, although most of them can be turned more easily, to the apparent summit pinnacle (cairn). The highest pt. is a little further, past two minor towers, to the next pinnacle with cairn (30 min.). Or: Cross the snowband to its upper R-hand end, above which two parallel couloir/chimneys rise to the ridge. Climb either to the crest which is reached about 5 min. from the 1st summit cairn (30 min., $3\frac{1}{4}$ h. from hut, $4\frac{3}{4}$ h. from Arolla).

Descent: From the true summit follow the crest to the first gendarme or slightly lower summit of S Peak. Just beyond this go down a small lateral crest to the L (E), or by a couloir between it and the main SW ridge. So reach the horizontal snowband. Make a descending traverse R (S) over this and reach the L side, looking down, of the couloir below Col Slingsby. Descend rib on the L side of the couloir to the top of a step where the gully to R seems to be vertical. Work down half R on very steep rock for a pitch then cross the gully to its R side. Go down the R side to steep snow at the bottom, where the slope broadens above the entry buttresses ($1\frac{3}{4}$ h., i.e. same time as in ascent).

South-West Ridge Complete. The ridge starts at saddle pt. 3264m. Rarely done in ascent, but the best way down after traversing the mtn. from N to S, especially for rte. finding in poor visibility or bad conditions. In this respect more straightforward and easier than Rte. 92, but slightly longer.

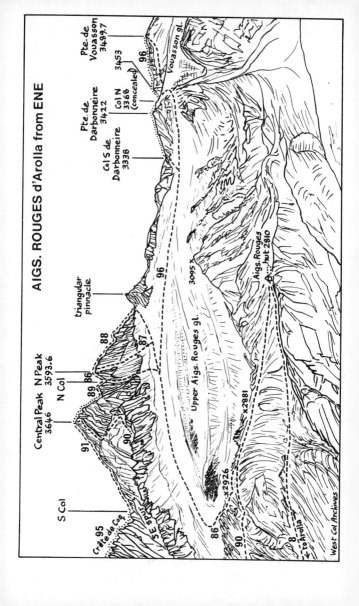

AIGS. ROUGES d'Arolla from ENE

Pte. de Vouasson 3489.7

Vouasson gl.

96

Col N 3453

Pte. de Darbonneire 3422

Col N 3368 (concealed)

Col S de Darbonneire 3338

96

Central Peak 3646

N Peak 3593.6

N Col

triangular pinnacle

88

87

86

89

96

3095 x

91

90

Upper Aigs. Rouges gl.

x 2881

S Col

S E S~~~

Crête de Coq 95

86

x 2926

Aigs. Rouges hut 2810

90

8

to Arolla

West Col Archives

PD. The ESE ridge of pt. 3486m., called La Mangette, is steeper and more difficult (R. W. Brant, R. Cory, W. Larden, 26 June, 1897). First ascent: F. W. Olliver with A. Georges, P. Maître, 16 August, 1892.

93 From the Aigs. Rouges hut follow Rtes. 86, 90 to the Lower Aigs. Rouges gl. Descend a little across this S and pass below the ESE ridge of pt. 3486m. Ascend moraine in a hollow then a snow slope without incident to a narrow rockband under saddle 3264m., which is easily reached ($2\frac{1}{4}$ h. from hut, $3\frac{3}{4}$ h. from Arolla). Follow the easy ridge with pleasant scrambling to pt. 3486m., descend a little over a snow saddle to continue over a ridge hump with a few small pinnacles and a short wall leading down to Col Slingsby (1 h.) where Rte. 92 is joined (30 min. to summit, $3\frac{3}{4}$ h. from hut, $5\frac{1}{4}$ h. from Arolla).

East Face Direct. A fine climb on mostly good rock. The intermediate gullies are loose. 520m. D-, pitches of IV+ and one of V. 10 pegs used on first ascent: D. & L. Louvel, 28 August, 1972.

94 From the Aigs. Rouges hut reach the foot of the North Couloir at the head of the Lower Aigs. Rouges gl. by Rtes. 86, 90 ($1\frac{1}{2}$ h.). In the base of the E face, just L of the couloir foot at 3060m. is a secondary snow gully cutting R. A big grey dièdre rises just L of its opening. Ascend a steep snow cone into the secondary gully and climb it for 30m. to another, parallel dièdre on the L. Get into this (IV+) and climb it (III) to exit by a little chimney (III+) and belay on top of a small pillar. Above, climb a red wall direct by a thin crack (35m., IV+, exposed). At the top descend 5m. then climb trending L for 70m. below overhanging rock (III). Continue directly up an obvious buttress, turning an overhang on the R (V), from where a series of gullies bearing R lead (II) to a bigger gully which is crossed R. Work round the buttress on its R, then climb the next buttress for 50m. (III) until a move R can be made on to a parallel continuation buttress/rib. Follow this for 70m. to finish up its E crest directly to summit of S Peak ($4\frac{1}{2}$ h. from gully entrance).

North-East Ridge (from South Col). This is the pièce de résistance of the Aigs. Rouges, and is known locally as the Crête de Coq. Perfect rock. The crest forms 15 gendarmes, a 16th marking the summit. Some of them can be avoided on the L (E) side but it is preferable to stay on or near the crest. There are several easier variations some distance down on the E face. In descent the best rte. is not easy to find and a lazy party will resort to numerous abseils. AD+, sustained, pitches of III, IV and moves of IV+. Descended by the first ascensionists. Ascended with long traverses on E flank by T. Brushfield, J. Collier, W. C. Compton, H. Owen, A. V. Valentine-Richards with 4 guides, 14 August, 1897.

95 From South Col the 1st gendarme is climbed easily. Work up to 10m. below the top of 2nd, on the L (E) side, and continue along a horizontal ledge which finishes in a steep enclosed gully overlooking the gl. below. Care is required to find the proper way at this pt. Follow ledge until you are below gap between the 2nd and 3rd gendarmes. Climb through a tunnel rock till you can see the gl. on the other (W) side. Looking at the 4th gendarme, a large flake can be seen on its E face, below the top. This is the original Crête de Coq. The flake is not sufficiently detached to enable you to jam up it. Start on its crest with a small overhang, then climb direct (IV+) to a scree ledge. Follow ledge for 15m. (cairn), then climb to a small parallel rib which descends E from the 5th gendarme. Climb this rib to foot of the gendarme, which can be turned on L, but it is preferable to follow a ledge on the R. Better still, climb the vertical 15m. wall to top of the gendarme on small but good holds (IV), and descend to the next gap.

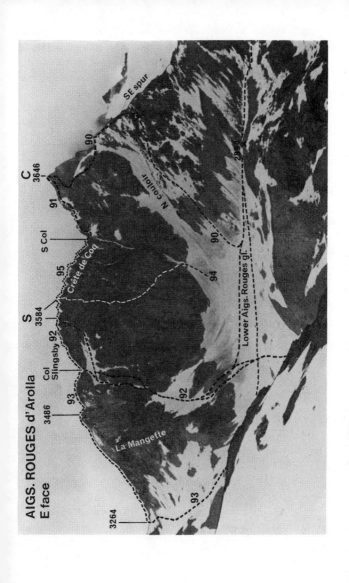

AIGS. ROUGES d'Arolla
E face

SE spur
90
C 3646
91
N couloir
S Col
90
95
Crête de Coq
94
S 3584
Lower Aigs. Rouges gl.
Col Slingsby 92
92
93
3486
La Mangette
93
3264

From the gap climb a short overhang (IV+, crux) at the base of the 6th gendarme, followed by a wall on small holds (5m., IV). Reach the top of the gendarme and follow the exposed knife-edge crest which is not particularly difficult to the 7th Gendarme. Continue to the foot of the 8th, from where you trend L on the E side, with an overhanging move to start, followed by slabs with small holds (IV). Reach the constricted gap between the 8th and 9th. Climb the latter by trending L, then descend easily to the next and largest gap in the ridge. From here descend a few m. on the L side, then climb a wide crack for 8m. (III) to a small scree platform. Now climb a slab direct (III) to the top of the 10th. Traverse the 11th without difficulty. The 12th is climbed by a large crack and loose rock on the L side. The 13th by a short vertical wall. The 14th and 15th are easy. The 16th lands you on the summit.

This is the most direct rte. ($2\frac{1}{3}$-$3\frac{1}{2}$ h. from South Col). There are easier variations, by which the ridge can be climbed in $1\frac{1}{2}$-2 h., up and down gullies and across ramps and short walls with chimney/cracks on E face.

North-South Traverse. See introduction to Aigs. Rouges as a whole. A superb expedition, classic and very popular. Some of the overhanging gendarmes on the Crête de Coq section, Rte. 95, which are described as turned, are in fact climbed by many parties; adds 2 or 3 pitches of IV+/V, notably at the 3rd and 4th gendarmes, the latter being the crux. Otherwise the traverse is AD- with the Crête de Coq section AD+. The first complete traverse is unknown. When it was first done fairly frequently most parties chose the easier S-N direction. One of the first was: E. Chadwick with P. Bernet, C. Jossi, 28 June, 1897. From N-S (without N Peak) by party named in Rte. 95.

Today most parties start from North Col (i. e. do not traverse the N Peak) and finish at Col Slingsby (i. e. do not continue over

108

pt. 3486m.). The rte. links for this are as follows:

Rte. 86 to North Col (2 h.), 89 to Central Peak ($1\frac{1}{2}$ h.), 91 to South Col (30 min.), 95 to S Peak ($1\frac{1}{2}$-$3\frac{1}{2}$ h. according to line taken), 92 to Col Slingsby and foot of mtn. ($1\frac{3}{4}$ h.), then back to hut (1 h.), or return to Arolla. Total time without halts, 8-10 h., allow at least 12 h.

If, as is proper, the complete ridge is done, you add at the start the traverse of the N Peak, Rtes. 88, 86, and finish by Rte. 93. This adds about 3 h. to the previous total.

POINTE DE VOUASSON 3489.7m.

LK 1326. A popular alternative outing for visitors to the Aigs. Rouges hut. Fine viewpoint. Rpt. Talbot, 1974. First known ascent: A. de Torrenté, F.O. Wolf, X. Wuilloud with M. Mabillard, P. Vuigner, 18 June, 1868.

From East. A pleasant snow excursion with easy scrambling. The gl. slopes can become icy after mid season. F+.

96 From the Aigs. Rouges hut follow Rte. 86 to below the N Peak of the Aigs. Rouges. Traverse horizontally N over the gl. to scree and rubble under the minor Pte. de Darbonneire. Now either traverse round its E spur to a steep little wing of the Vouasson gl. to the N, and go up this to level snow beside the Col N de Darbonneire (3368m.); or traverse the ridges of the Pte. from its S col to N col. From the N col cross snow/ scree NW and either climb the easy SE rock ridge, or reach this ridge closer to the summit from the upper snowfields of the Vouasson gl. ($3\frac{3}{4}$ h. from hut).

Cheilon - Pleureur - Rosablanche Chain

COL DE LA SERPENTINE   3547m.

97 LK 1346. Between La Serpentine and Mt. Blanc de Cheilon, this pass is used as a means of access to the E ridge of the Cheilon. See Rte. 102. As a pass between the Dix and Chanrion huts, it is long and crevassed. PD. First crossed by A. W. Moore, H. Walker with J. Anderegg, 9 July, 1865.

LA SERPENTINE N. 3795m.   S. 3712.9m.

98 LK 1346. Huge whaleback mass of rock and ice dividing the Serpentine and Brenay gl. Easily climbed from slopes adjoining the Brenay (Rte. 83) and Serpentine (Rte. 102) cols. First recorded ascent: E. Hoffmann-Burkhardt with S. Bessard, J. Fellay, 16 July, 1866.

MONT BLANC DE CHEILON   3869.8m.

LK 1346. The quaint name signifies milkpail. Undoubtedly the finest rock and ice mtn. in the Arolla district. It has a fairly complex structure with rock and ice ridges radiating like the spokes of a wheel. These ridges carry two distinct forepeaks of the same measured height (3827m.), SE and SW. The mtn. has an impressive profile when seen from the N, from the Dix hut. This side, 1 h. walk from hut, has all the majesty and severity of any 4000m. summit in the Pennines. Although the distance looks forbidding, the mtn. is climbed fairly often from the Chanrion hut. The ascent is equally possible from the Vignettes hut by traversing the Pigne d'Arolla. The S and W flanks are of no special interest, but they offer the easiest ways up and down. The classic traverse by the E and W ridges is one of the best expeditions of its class in the Pennine Alps. Rpt. Talbot, 1974; Anstruther, 1978.
    First ascent: J. J. Weilenmann with J. Fellay, 11 September, 1865. Second ascent (British): F. C. Fitton with F. & M. Payot, 18 July, 1866 (from Chanrion).

MT. BLANC DE CHEILON from SW
3869.8

AIGS. ROUGES

102
3827
3869.8
3827
101
101 var.
108
101

<u>West-North-West Flank (from Col de Cheilon)</u>. The usual rte. and the best descent from the mtn. A pleasant, interesting and very popular excursion. F+/PD. The pass is an important connection between the Dix and Chanrion huts and was formerly used as a direct way from Arolla to Mauvoisin. F. First ascensionists.

99 From the Dix hut descend to the Cheilon gl. and walk up its moraines (track) on R (N) side to snow/ice slopes which are followed without possible error to the Col de Cheilon (3243m.) (1 h.).

100 From the Chanrion hut a small path with cairns leads N to a jeep trail, crossed at pt. 2522m. Continue N above this trail, then the track bends R (NE) and mounts a moraine (2624m.) below the Brenay gl. Follow moraine until a lateral moraine ridge can be crossed L near the lower end of the gl., bare ice, which is then crossed to the opposite N side with more moraine piles, directly under a rocky spur coming down from pt. 3074.2m., some distance R of the tarns marked pt. 2721m., which cannot be seen. Cross stones to join a track mounting due N and turning the foot of the aforementioned spur on the R. Follow track to the wide saddle of the <u>Col de Lire Rose</u> (3115m.) at the top (2¼ h.).

Descend slightly to the N, cross snowfields of the tiny Lire Rose gl., and climb a fairly steep snow/rubble slope due N to the <u>Col du Mt. Rouge</u> (3325m.) (30 min.). A short snow/ice wall frequently forms below this col. It can normally be avoided by a very steep rope length at the W end. Now walk almost horizontally NE across the vast snowfield of the Giétro gl., below the Ruinette, to the Col de Cheilon. Beware of masked crevasses after mid season (45 min., 3½ h. from Chanrion hut, 4¼ h. to Dix hut; in reverse direction from Dix to Chanrion huts, 3½ h.).

In practice, when coming from the Chanrion hut to climb Mt. Blanc de Cheilon, it is not necessary to go right across the snowfield to the Col de Cheilon (see below).

101 From the Col de Cheilon climb an obvious rock ridge, or use snow slopes on its S side, but return to ridge halfway up this section. From the ridge top climb direct on a broad snow/ice rib to a saddle (3785m.) in the SW ridge. A large bergschrund sometimes forms below this saddle, in which case avoid it by moving further R to reach the snowcap of the SW forepeak (3827m.) (2 h.). Now follow the snow crest of the SW ridge, sometimes heavily corniced on R (S) side, or with hard ice, to a short rock section leading directly to summit (45 min., $2\frac{3}{4}$ h. from col, $3\frac{3}{4}$ h. from Dix hut; $6\frac{1}{4}$ h. from Chanrion hut).

Chanrion variation (2nd ascensionists). Having passed the foot of the NW face of the Ruinette (pt. 3361m.), from the Giétro snowfield ascend a broad gl. band to the E with several large crevasses, which slants below the N side ice slope of the NE ridge of the Ruinette. Near the top easy snow slopes lead in a crescent N to the snowcap forepeak (3827m.). Then as for the Col de Cheilon approach. Less steep than the corresponding section from latter col, and 30 min. shorter when coming from the Chanrion hut.

East Ridge (from Col de la Serpentine). Normally taken in ascent, for making a traverse of the mtn. Fine mixed climbing, PD+. First ascent: A. Macnamara, H.W. Topham with J. Maître, 7 September, 1887.

102 From the Dix hut follow Rte. 83 as for the Col de Brenay. On reaching the broad gl. spur above the Tsena Réfien gl., continue up this spur SW with a few large crevasses to the Col de la Serpentine (3547m.) ($2\frac{1}{2}$ h.). Coming from the Vignettes hut over the Pigne d'Arolla reach the col by descending

113

Rte. 83, finally with a slight deviation (3 h.).

From the col ascend snow L of crest line to avoid crevasses, and reach broken rocks forming the top of a rockband below S side of ridge. Work up these rocks for 10 min., then make a rising traverse R up a snow slope to an almost level part atop the ridge. Now follow the crest, often with big cornices to R, to the snowcap SE forepeak (3827m.). If the ridge is very icy, continue following the parallel upper edge of rocks on S side, and on reaching an obvious shoulder bear R up easy snow to forepeak. From here move L (S) and descend a rock step on this side, then traverse L and turn two small pinnacles. Return to the ridge immediately by a rising traverse L. Follow the crest over or round numerous short pinnacles and towers to a mini snow saddle, then similar climbing on the steeper summit ridge, all sound rock with pitches of II, to the top, ($2\frac{1}{2}$ h., 5 h. from Dix hut, $5\frac{1}{2}$ h. from Vignettes hut).

North-North-West (Gallet) Ridge. This ridge has enjoyed a curious fashionable reputation, borne out neither by popularity nor quality, both of which are lacking in any real sense. Its reputation seems to have been made by observers rather than by people who have actually done the climb. As to quality, Gardner remarked, "the rocks are loose and of the very worst description", while Talbot as recently as 1974 noted, "a large accumulation of loose rock of all sizes all along the upper part of the ridge". Despite the "facts", the ridge is climbed more often than the complementary Jenkins ridge, and the modern climber is more inured in pyschological techniques for overcoming bad rock. Snow and ice on the ridge is common; in the right sort of icy conditions the loose rock is undoubtedly made safer as several correspondents have reported. If the best way up the ridge can be found there are no pitches harder than III. The rte. is variable. Overall grading in good conditions, rare for this ridge, AD+. 600m. First ascent:

J. Gallet with A. Bovier father & son, 20 July, 1896. Descended by H. M. Gardner with A. Bovier son, A. Georges, 25 July, 1905. In winter: G. Jordan with C. Bournissen, 11 January, 1964. Winter solo: J. F. Moix, 3 January, 1975.

103 From the Dix hut descend to the Cheilon gl. and walk up its R (N) side to c. 3000m. Now cross the gl. SE, crevasses in same direction, and reach the obvious saddle at the foot of the ridge, behind pt. 3226m. (1 h.). Follow the crest precisely for the first 200m., to a zone of large steep slabs. These rise into a pyramid forming a large red tower, about halfway up the ridge. Climb slabs near their L side, normally icy, and take a large snow/ice patch on L side of the base of the red tower. Get into a chimney/gully system between subsidiary pillars on L side of tower and follow this system for several pitches, some of them on snow/ice, to near the small gap behind the top of the tower. Keep L below a small tower section on the crest, up an icy rock gully, to join the crest at a slabby step. Climb this on the crest or just L of it to a small gap, and continue up the next step for a steep pitch to where the upper ridge eases off a little. Now follow the crest as closely as possible with large masses of wedged rock poised on the crest to the summit (5 h., 6 h. from hut).

North-North-East (Jenkins) Ridge. Longer and more varied than the Gallet ridge, and technically more difficult. 750m., AD+ with pitches of III+. First ascent: A. S. Jenkins with J. Bournissen, J. Gaudin, 20 July, 1905. Descended by Mlle. M. Gerber with B. & C. Bournissen, 19 August, 1934. In winter: M. Petermann, P. Thélin, 13 January, 1973. Winter solo: R. Moix, January, 1974.

104 From the Dix hut cross the gl. directly to the foot of the ridge (45 min.). The ridge foot is a wall. Turn it L on steep broken ice, sometimes complicated, then climb a snow/ice slope parallel to ridge, cross the bergschrund and slant R on ice to the ridge flank where sound rocks enable the crest to be reached. Follow the crest with pitches of III on reasonable rock to the middle snowy section. A narrow rib of poor rock is pursued as directly as possible with short icy movements L to reach a section of 4 short towers of unrelenting steepness. These lead to a sloping snow crest under a big narrow tower. (This tower has been climbed direct at grade IV/V). Traverse diagonally R up a short rockband, below a higher and more obvious ramp, on to steep mixed ground under R side of tower and high above the N face couloir. Work close to the tower wall by 2 or 3 awkward pitches to a wall on the L, under the gap behind the tower and below a gully straight ahead. Climb this wall, often icy (crux), to the gap. The last section above gap is climbed for 2 rope lengths to a broad buttress under the summit. Go up the L side of this to the top (5-6 h. from bergschrund).

North Face. A big competitive climb, probably the most important of its kind in the Western Pennines. The face is a huge ice couloir with a large headwall at the top, contained between the converging arms of the Gallet and Jenkins ridges. Not counting minor variations, four different lines have been taken up the face, due mainly to parties being forced off a direct ascent by poor conditions. At the end of a dry season a great deal of smooth rock is exposed, leaving only a narrow ice ribbon in the bed. There is always some stonefall danger, but in good conditions, especially in early season, this is negligible. Climbing times have varied tremendously. The first ascensionists bivouacked and altogether took 30 h. On the other hand several parties have climbed the face in under 4 h. 650m., TD-/TD, average angle 54°, steeper in the upper half. Comparable with the Triolet N face. Climbed 10 times up to 1965 and frequently since then.

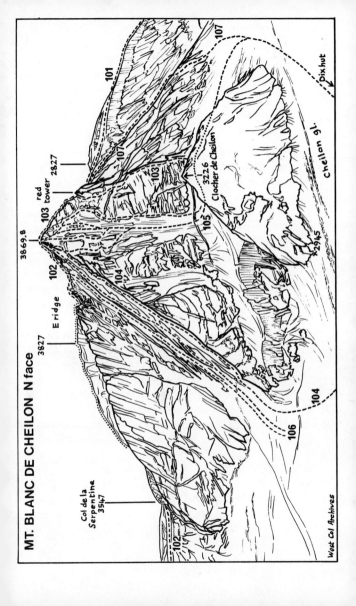

MT. BLANC DE CHEILON N face

Col de la Serpentine 3547

3827

E ridge

3869.8

102

red tower 103

2827

101

107

107

103

3226

Clocher de Cheilon

105

Dix hut

107

Cheilon gl.

2945

104

104

106

102

West Col Archives

First ascent: W. Gorter, L. Steinauer, 28-29 September, 1938. Second: J. Rossier, E. Wolf, 24 July, 1951 ($5\frac{1}{2}$ h. from hut). In winter: S. Jenny, H. Wagner, 21 February, 1965 ($8\frac{1}{2}$ h., by R-hand side with exit on to Gallet ridge 150m. below summit). R-hand side rocks followed to direct exit: G. Albisser, F. Haechler, 4 October, 1959. Upper L rib variant: R. Bögli, L. Favre, 2 September, 1963. First British ascent: B. Clark, D. Haston, September, 1971 (by Upper L rib variant).

105 Reach the foot of the face by crossing the saddle under the Gallet ridge, Rte. 103 (1 h. from Dix hut). Cross the bergschrund and climb the ice slope in the centre of the couloir. More than halfway up there is a vague but broader branch slope to R, which returns L above the steepest section of the couloir proper. The direct ascent at this pt. is close to the L retaining rock spur and is very steep, with narrows and a rock pitch of IV, depending on snow conditions, then a runnelled slope and longer narrows, normally taken by a rib just R, to the first rockbands under the summit. Ascend the rockbands trending L in a gully line with pitches of IV/IV+ (without a lot of good snow, V) directly to summit. This section can be avoided by a slightly easier R-hand movement across shallow gullies and ribs to join the Gallet ridge on R some 50m. from top (6-9 h. from bergschrund).

R-hand side rocks. Climb rocks bordering this side of central couloir, up to the R-hand couloir branch. Cross the top of this L, ascend two rockbands and continue diagonally L under a narrow buttress towards the normal direct exit. Finish R of the gully on very steep smooth snowy slabs (several pitches of V).

Upper L rib variant. Just below the first narrows in the central couloir, climb snowy rocks on to the L retaining rock spur. Follow this with increasing difficulties to the summit. The rocks become very awkward if covered with a lot of snow. Pegs for protection. This variation is attractive and advantageous when the upper part of the couloir is in poor condition.

Outer L rib variant. Immediately below the origin of the rib bordering the upper part of the couloir, trend L on snow/ice to a higher and narrower rock rib which further up bends L towards the Jenkins ridge. From the ice get on to this rib with difficulty and follow it for several unprotected pitches to a snow/ice band at a higher level. Climb this steeply and by trending L reach the rockband extending R from the base of the narrow tower near the top of the Jenkins ridge; so join this rte. by a very difficult traverse L, to finish. Pointless except as an escape rte.

106 North-East Face. Three uneven low relief rock ribs rise up L (E) of the Jenkins ridge, the R-hand one merging into the ridge about two-thirds way up. "Not a pretty sight, so you can keep it" (Haston). The first party climbed a shallow gully line L of the L-hand rib, moving on to the rib at two-thirds height, and finished on the E ridge, it is stated, about 60m. below summit. However, this place is a little snow neck at c. 3790m., some 80m. below and 100m. distant from summit. Mixed climbing with loose rock and threatened by falling ice from the huge E ridge cornice. D+. J.V. Anthoine, W.G. Barker, K. Nannery, 4-5 March, 1973 (ACG Bull. 1973-4, pp. 23-24). Second ascent by central rib, exiting directly on to the final buttress of Jenkins ridge, with similar climbing and several pitches of IV. J.F. & R. Moix, 31 December, 1975 - 1 January, 1976.

107 North-West Face. This lies on the R side of the Gallet ridge and consists of a series of low relief rock ribs merging into a pyramid under the summit. The rte. follows the R-hand rib, starting up the first subsidiary rib 60m. L of this at the bottom (to avoid stone and ice fall further R), and joins the main rib where it steepens. Mixed climbing, mostly on poor rock with a few sound pitches of IV. Described as comparable with the Jenkins ridge. 650m., D-. First ascent: G. Genoud, M. Pétermann, 29 December, 1973 (8 h.).

Cheilon-Ruinette Ridge. Nearly $2\frac{1}{2}$ km. long this fine traverse is the most serious undertaking of its kind in the Dix basin area. Exceptional situations but rarely done. Easier in the Ruinette-Cheilon direction. Only the NE ridge proper of La Ruinette has considerable technical difficulties. However, glazed rocks and huge cornices are common to the frequent poor conditions on this ridge. AD+ with a section of IV. In reverse direction, AD-, by abseiling. First traverse: F. W. Oliver with A. Georges, P. Maître, 15 September, 1893 ($4\frac{1}{2}$ h.).

108 From the summit of Mt. Blanc de Cheilon follow the rocky then snowy ridge into saddle 3785m. and over snowcap forepeak 3827m. to a snow depression where a long section of narrow rock crest commences. Continue on the broken crest with generally poor rock but no obstacles to another saddle (3696m.) at the end of this section. The next part is more or less horizontal and gradually becomes a sharp snow/ice crest with a large cornice developing on S side. It rises to a few rock teeth then a rockhead and shoulder leading into the final very steep ridge step before the Ruinette summit ($2\frac{1}{2}$ h.). Follow the progressively steepening rock crest, often icy and snow plastered, to a series of small red rock teeth. Climb or turn these by short traverses, delicate and exposed, up to the last and most formidable gendarme. Move up R on the NW side to the foot of a broad, near vertical chimney. Climb the bed, loose and icy (IV) to the top of the gendarme, cross the gap behind it, followed by a short ridge to the summit ($1\frac{1}{2}$-$2\frac{1}{2}$ h., 4-5 h. from Mt. Blanc de Cheilon).

Note: The last gendarme has been climbed up its L(E) side by cracked slabs and walls; no details but rumoured to be

120

preferable to the original chimney.

LA RUINETTE   3875m.

LK 1346.   A striking rock peak, the highest pt. between the
Dents d'Hérens and the Grand Combin. Generally poor rock
but most of the climbing is on mixed terrain. A popular excursion. Rpt. Talbot, 1974. First ascent: E. Whymper with
C. Almer, F. Biner, 6 July, 1865. Second: J.J. Weilenmann
with J.M. Rosso, 6 September, 1865.

<u>South-West Ridge</u>.   The usual way to the summit, variable
approaches according to conditions on the mtn.   PD. First
ascensionists.

109 From the Chanrion hut reach the Brenay gl. as for Rte. 100.
Work up the medial moraine of this gl. to c. 2820m. then slant
across it to the N bank at c. 2860m. Climb scree slopes N and
NW, some distance S (L) of pt. 3050. 3m., to reach the lower
edge of the Ruinette gl. by smooth rocks, on the S side of the
mtn.   Climb direct (NW) over crevassed slopes to reach the
SW ridge at a wide snow saddle forming the lowest pt. between
pt. 3710m. on L (W) and summit on R. Now go up the ridge
with steep loose scrambling to the summit (5 h. from Chanrion
hut).   After mid season the Ruinette gl. becomes very crevassed and icy.

110 From the Chanrion hut, the most direct and shortest approach which mostly avoids trouble with bad snow and crevasses, but has some steep unpleasant rocks.
   Reach the Col du Mt. Rouge as for Rte. 100 ($2\frac{3}{4}$ h.). This
is also the easiest approach from the Dix hut, by taking Rte. 99
then 100 in reverse ($1\frac{1}{4}$ h.). From the col climb the steep broad
ridge to the E, and reach the rockhead pt. 3710m. There are
several ways up this broad ridge. (a) By the crest direct,
scree and blocks for 100m. at a high angle, often dangerous,

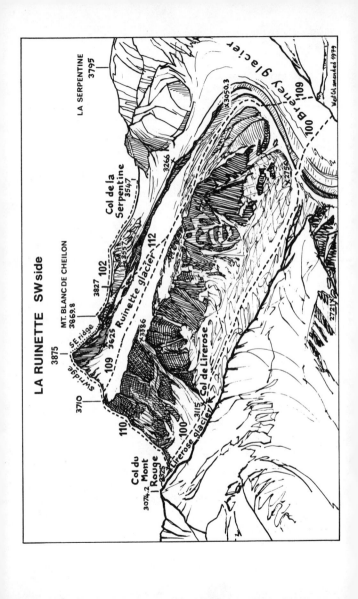

LA RUINETTE SW side

LA SERPENTINE
3795

Breney glacier

600

100

Welch amended 1979

x3050.3

Col de la
Serpentine
3547

3266

3557

Col de la Serpentine

3827   102

Ruinette glacier 112

2756

MT. BLANC DE CHEILON
3869.8

3875

SE ridge

SW ridge

109   3625   x3386

110   110

3710

Col du
Mont
Rouge
3074.2

Col de Lirerose

Lirerose glacier   3115
100

2721

cold and possibly icy during the morning; then by equally steep but better rocks, and snow patches. (b) By the rock wall immediately R (S) of the broad ridge. (c) By a broad snow couloir slope on the L (N) side; this is probably the best and quickest way if the snow is good ($1\frac{1}{4}$ h.). From pt. 3710m. follow the ridge over saddle as for Rte. 109 (1 h., 5 h. from Chanrion hut, 4 h. from Dix hut).

<u>North-East Ridge</u>. See Rte. 108. The ridge can be reached from the gl. crescent variation (Chanrion) of Rte. 101, at the snow saddle just S of pt. 3827m.

<u>North-West Face</u>. A broad, fairly symmetrical wall of rock ribs with a complicated climbing history. At least 8 lines have been taken to the main ridge, extending as far out as the upper rockhead shoulder below the NE ridge, to pt. 3710m. on the SW ridge. The rib starting from a pt. c.50m. along the SW ridge from summit, running down to pt. 3380m., was climbed by C. Berthet, E. W. Viollier, A. Ybloux with J. Quinodoz, August, 1888. PD, loose, stonefall, not recommended. The last long rib at the R side of the face, well shown on map, joining the SW ridge about 250m. distance from summit, was descended by W. W. Naismith with J. Quinodoz, 16 August, 1895. PD, broken rock on a very narrow low relief rib, starting 75m. above the bergschrund. Slight stonefall danger, the easiest and quickest way up the face (2 h.). The next main rib L of this rte. is described below. The rib descending from the last gendarme on the NE ridge, just L of summit, and forming a pear shaped buttress at the bottom, being the L-hand of two such buttresses, was climbed up its L side (AD+) and again on its R side, keeping R of upper rib in the central couloir (TD), in 1970.

The best line on the face is the first continuous rib L of the 1895 descent rte. Fairly free from stonefall once you are es-

tablished on the rib. PD+ with pitches of III. Rock quite good.
First ascent: J. L. Belton, D. Norton, 1 August, 1965.

111 Reach the foot of the face from the Dix or Chanrion huts
by Rtes. 99, 100 in $1\frac{1}{2}$ h. or 3 h. respectively. Start R of the
summit line below a double rib situated 125m. distance diagonally R from pt. 3380m. There are gendarmes on the upper
L-hand part. To the immediate R is a snow/ice slope dividing
the double rib from the last continuous long rib on the face
(1895 rte.). Cross the bergschrund and climb a steep snow/
ice slope to the L-hand part of the double rib. Go up direct,
first on poor rock, which soon improves and gives good climbing with pitches of III. If required, the gendarmes can be
turned on the R. The rib finishes on the SW ridge about 120m.
from the summit (4 h., $5\frac{1}{2}$ h. from Dix hut, 7 h. from Chanrion
hut).

112 <u>South-East Ridge.</u> If the Ruinette gl. is in good condition,
Rte. 109, it can be ascended to an obvious snow slope leading
on to this ridge above pt. 3557m., from where the crest is
followed on broken rock, steeper than the SW ridge, to top.
PD (5 h. from Dix hut). Second ascensionists in descent.

POINTE D'OTEMMA 3403.2m.

LK 1346. Fine rock pyramid. A popular training climb situated
immediately E of the Chanrion hut. Mostly sound rock. First
tourist ascent: J. J. Weilenmann with J. Gillioz, 23 July, 1866.

<u>West Ridge.</u> The usual rte., and the shortest way up. Good
rock, II.

113 From the Chanrion hut follow a clearly marked track N,
crossing a jeep trail, to a grassy shoulder below the ridge.
Go up shoulder to foot of ridge. Ascend an opening between
two small bluffs to a stony crest on L. The initial ridge above

is in two steep sections taken on the crest, then a uniformly more broken upper crest to a slight shoulder and a short summit step (3 h. from hut).

Variation. A popular alternative is to work ENE from hut (tracks), to the foot of a couloir in the S flank of the ridge, reaching up to the top of the second steep section, about halfway up the ridge. When there is good snow in the couloir, this way is more useful for descent by steep glissading. Normally scree and loose rubble after mid season.

South Ridge. The best rte. for making a simple traverse of the mtn. Mostly II, short pitches of III. Some stonefall danger in the long approach couloir. Descended by Misses E. & M. & Mr. D. Wilkinson with A. Georges, J. Métrailler, 6 September, 1907.

114 From the Chanrion hut follow the upper traverse path leading to the Otemma gl. Where this turns sharp S to cross a series of grassy buttresses, climb the second grassy buttress directly above to a long screeband (snow) under W flank of S ridge. Above is the second ridge gap (3182m.) with a scree/rock/snow gully descending from it to the screeband. Climb the L-hand (N side) entrance to the gully and go up under a rock wall to where the subsidiary entrances converge. Now climb steep rocks on R side of the gully, as directly as possible, with short zigzag traverses, to reach the gap. The first ridge step has two good pitches followed by scrambling over a broken hump and into a small saddle/gap below the summit. Continue on the crest with interesting scrambling to the top ($3\frac{3}{4}$ h. from hut).

COL DE CHEILON 3243m.

LK 1346. An old gl. pass, frequented for two centuries. See Rtes. 99, 100.

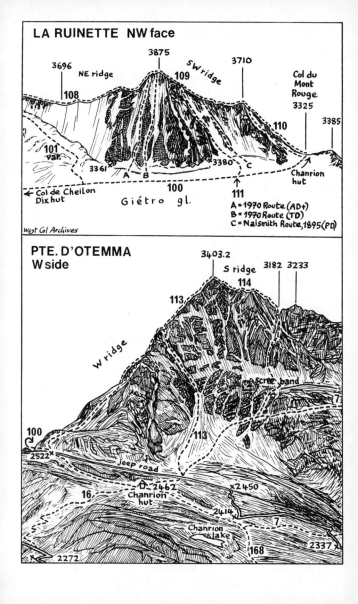

LA RUINETTE NW face

3696
NE ridge
3875
SW ridge
3710
Col du
Mont
Rouge
3325
109
108
3385
101 var.
3361
3380
C
Chanrion
hut
A B
Col de Cheilon
Dix hut
100
111
110
Giétro gl.

A = 1970 Route (AD+)
B = 1970 Route (TD)
C = Naismith Route, 1895 (PD)

West Col Archives

PTE. D'OTEMMA W side

3403.2
S ridge
3182 3233
114
113
W ridge
scree band
7
100
113
2522 x
Jeep road
16
2462
Chanrion hut
x 2450
2414
7
2272
Chanrion lake
168
2337 x
x

LA LUETTE   3548.3m.

LK 1346.   Popular training objective, a short day from the Dix hut.   First ascent unknown.   Rpt. Talbot, 1974.

East Side and South-East Ridge.   The usual rte., variable according to conditions.   F/F+.   First recorded ascent: C. Hauser, G. van De Poll, A. von Wattenwyl with H. Elmer and A. Gaspoz, 25 July, 1869.

115 From the Dix hut a small track climbs W to a grassy knoll then peters out in moraine beside the Luette gl. above pt. 2997m. Go on to the gl. where it is least crevassed, variable, and ascend WSW to a saddle in the SE ridge just behind snowcap pt. 3444m. and before rock outcrop pt. 3465m. Small bergschrund before saddle, and reach ridge at inner end, closer to pt. 3465m. because there is often a cornice/snow wall at L side.   From here follow easy snow and rock ridge to summit ($2\frac{1}{2}$ h. from hut).

If the Luette gl. is badly crevassed, take the track over moraine beside the Cheilon gl., towards the Col de Cheilon, and at c. 3020m. cut up R (WNW) over scree and rubble slopes to the S edge of the Luette gl.   Follow edge L (W) normally on easy snow to a slight saddle with outcrops S of snowcap pt. 3444m. on the SE ridge ($2\frac{1}{2}$ h.).

For the SE ridge complete, starting at the Col de Cheilon, Rte. 99 from Dix hut in 1 h., or from the Chanrion hut by Rte. 100 in $3\frac{1}{2}$ h., follow crest up scree, blocks and outcrops with two small rockheads to where the ridge is joined by the previous approaches (2 h., 3 h. from Dix hut, $5\frac{1}{2}$ h. from Chanrion hut).

When the Luette gl. is in good condition, much the quickest way down to the Dix hut is by the snow and rock slope forming E face.   From the summit go along the NE ridge for 50m., then cut down fairly steep snow R on to the face.   Work down near an edge of rocks on the L (N) side to a bergschrund and the gl. at the bottom ($1\frac{1}{4}$ h. to hut).

LE PLEUREUR   3703.5m.

LK 1346. An impressive mass of rock and ice with spectacular
cliffs on W side, overlooking Mauvoisin. Rock, schist and
generally poor. Most parties start from the Dix hut and return
the same way. A traverse continued over La Sale involves at
the end reascending the Dix hut path all the way from the bridge
at the S end of the Dix barrage lake. Rpt. Talbot, 1974. First
recorded ascent: E. Hoffmann-Burkhardt with S. Bessard, J.
Fellay, J. Gillioz, 13 July, 1866.

East-South-East (Luette-Pleureur) Ridge.   An interesting
mixed scramble, popular. PD. First ascent: E. Thury, L.
Wanner with J. H. Bessard, 16 August, 1884.

116 From the Dix hut follow one of the various ways in Rte. 115
to summit of La Luette ($2\frac{1}{2}$ h.). Now descend the main ridge
to the Col de la Luette (3368m.), on snow, generally corniced
(20-30 min.). Continue along ridge with a cornice R to a mainly
rocky part up to a schist knoll between two narrow snow crests.
A little higher reach a rock step which is turned on L side (S)
by ledges for three rope lengths. Return to the crest without
difficulty and reach the snowcap summit which is a few m.
higher than the measured cairn on an adjoining rock to W ($1\frac{1}{4}$ h.,
$4\frac{1}{4}$ h. from Dix hut, $7\frac{1}{4}$ h. from Chanrion hut. Half these times
in descent).

North Ridge (from La Sale).   Link in the traverse of the Pleureur group. Characteristic mixed ground. PD/PD+. First
ascent: J. H. Isler with J. Fellay, F. Gaba, 21 July, 1867.

117 From the summit of La Sale (see below) descend an easy
broken rock crest to snow saddle 3534m., then climb the rounded ridge step above, frequently icy, at 48° for 3 rope lengths
to a horizontal section and the summit (45 min. - $1\frac{1}{2}$ h.,

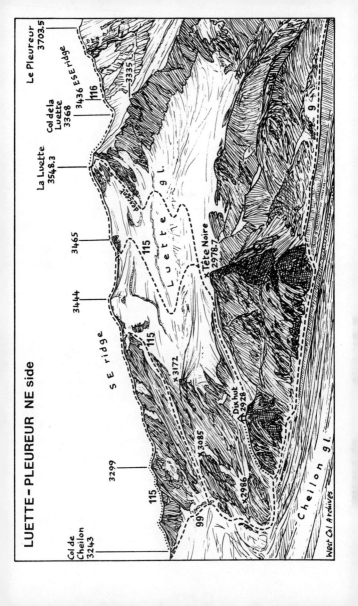

LUETTE – PLEUREUR NE side

Col de Cheilon 3243

S E ridge

3299

115

99

X 3085

X 3172

Dix hut 2928

X 2986

Cheilon gl.

115

115

3444

3465

Luette gl.

X Tête Noire 2978·7

115

La Luette 3548·3

Col de la Luette 3368

116

3436 ESE ridge

3335

Le Pleureur 3703·5

West Col Archives

according to snow/ice conditions, same time in reverse direction).

It appears that the rounded ridge step can be avoided by the steep but not often icy slopes of the Pleureur gl., crossing them horizontally S from the snow saddle to a pt. below the summit, followed by a direct ascent to the top.

Other Routes. Above the Mauvoisin barrage the SW ridge is fairly long, rarely climbed, but not difficult. The W face has an original rte. on loose rock, exposed to stonefall, which joins the SW ridge about 250m. from summit. Further L a direct rte. up the face, made in 1945, is characterised by friable overhanging rock and considerable technical difficulties (V).

LA SALE   3645.8m.

LK 1326, 1346.   Really a prominent satellite of Le Pleureur, normally traversed to reach the latter (see Rte. 117). The summit is a steep rock cone. First ascent: J. H. Isler with J. Gillioz, 27 August, 1866.

North-West Ridge (from Col du Vasevay).   In the context of the guidebook this col is reached when climbing the mtn. from the Pantalons Blancs biv. hut. A fairly short but interesting snow/ice rte. The key slope tends to be crevassed and icy. PD.   First ascensionists. Starting up this ridge, the first traverse by Rte. 117 to Le Pleureur (followed in this instance by a descent of the S face of Le Pleureur) seems to have been made by G. E. Foster, A. W. Moore with J. Anderegg, H. Baumann, 19 July, 1871.

118 From the Pantalons Blancs biv. hut traverse the easy snow slopes of the Pantalons Blancs gl. to S, rising a little over a broad snow spur coming out from the Pte. des Chamois (3384m.), and working along snow under its S ridge, as if aiming for the Pte. du Vasevay (3356m.). So reach a rubble terrace which slants across E side of this peak about 60m. below its summit, by which you reach in a few min. the lower rocks on S side of same peak, some 25m. above the Col du Vasevay (3225m.) (30 min.). From the col go up schist and snow (crevasses) beside the ridge crest to a steep snow/ice slope where the Sale gl. narrows. Climb the slope direct for 3 rope lengths. Normally attempts to turn the slope L (E) become entangled with bad crevasses. In a dry season this slope may be found as bare rock, and is then easy. Above, a moderate snow slope leads to a broad snow shoulder under the summit cone. Facing you, climb this by a 30m. chimney (II), sometimes icy and awkward for the first 10m. ($1\frac{1}{2}$-2 h., 2-$2\frac{1}{2}$ h. from biv. hut).

East Flank. An important descent rte. after traversing the Pleureur group. PD-. First climbed as the easiest way from the Hérémence (Dix) valley to La Sale, about 1890.

119 From the summit descend the rock edifice by a 30m. chimney (II) on N side and follow the broad snow dome above the NW ridge for a few min. to the N, then gradually bear R, going down in a circle to the E and ESE on a snow shoulder. Just before this ends move R into the head of a steep snow/rock gully facing E, which descends under pt. 3319m. At the bottom exit trending L down rough slopes of L'En Darrey, aiming to pass R of the little tarn on the grassy Plan de la Gouille and just R of pt. 2549m. further R (E), where grass slopes lead down to the bridge (2386m.) at the S end of the Dix lake, near the Pas du Chat ($1\frac{1}{2}$ h. in descent). Below the gully there are various tracks all the way down. Return to hut ($1\frac{1}{2}$ h.), or descend to barrage, as for Rte. 9.

Pleureur group traverse. A very fine expedition, highly recommended, mixed climbing, all kinds of terrain. PD+.

Starting from and returning to the Dix hut, by Rtes. 115, 116, 117, 9, some 8 h. without halts. First recorded British traverse thus: H. R. C. Carr, G. Lister, 26 July, 1923.

LE PARRAIN   3259.3m.

120 LK 1326. Small rock peak detached W of the main ridge in vicinity of the Pantalons Blancs biv. hut. Climbed from here via the easy Col du Crêt (3144m.), the obvious short connecting ridge to snow on N side of summit, then up rocks of its E facet. F. $1\frac{1}{4}$ h. from biv. hut.   First recorded ascent: S. Miney, E. W. Viollier, 2 August, 1890. Climbed by E. F. M. Benecke, H. A. Cohen, 12 July, 1894 - the pair who scandalised climbing ethics of the day by their guideless and solo exploits, and who disappeared the following year in mysterious circumstances while climbing - it is not known where exactly - near the head of the Lötschental.

LA ROSABLANCHE   3336.3m.

LK 1326. Outstanding secondary snow peak with magnificent regional views.   Very popular spring skiing excursion.   Due to new huts opened in the 1960s and 70s easily climbed from four directions. Rpt. Anstruther, 1978. First recorded ascent: J. J. Weilenmann with J. Fellay, 10 September, 1865. First British ascent: A. Cust, J. B. Parish with X. Andermatten, 12 August, 1882.

<u>From North-East (Prafleuri)</u>. A pleasant gl. walk, short, F. Can be done from top of Dix barrage cableway in half a day - thus by many mtn. walkers.

121 From the Prafleuri hut (1 h. above Dix cableway) a track, not shown on map, mounts SW for 10 min. , crossing the longer bends of a jeep road on a series of terraces. Join this road where it traverses NW then leave it after 5 min. , at the stream coming down from the Prafleuri gl. Follow the stream steeply to the snow/ice slope of the gl. tongue, under the Miroir. Work up the gl. , first trending R then near its centre over moderate slopes, towards the N side of the summit at the top, crevasses in late season. Reach the NE summit ridge by keeping slightly L and about 150m. distance from the top, then go up rocks and snow to summit (2 h. from hut, 1 h. in descent).

When the lower gl. tongue is icy, continue along the main trail N and NW until below the last riser to the Col de Prafleuri. This pt. can be reached more directly from the hut by a track going fairly directly up to pt. 2785m. Now go over moraine SW on to the W side of the gl., under the Mt. Calme ridge, and follow up near this side with few crevasses to the section under N side of summit (20 min. longer).

From South-East (Ecoulaies). The most interesting approach to the mtn., varied terrain, PD-. Unfortunately it involves a descent of 400m. at the outset, and parties can accomplish this approach from the Barma chalet (2458m.) on the Dix hut approach in much the same time, from where you also have the choice of taking the somewhat shorter Mourti gl. to col 3196m. under the summit ($3\frac{1}{4}$ h.).

122 From the Pantalons Blancs biv. hut make a slightly descending traverse W across the large gl. spur on which the hut rock island stands, then descend returning sharp R (NE) to avoid a crevassed step in the Ecoulaies gl., crevasses in same direction, and further down pass below a rock spur adjoining the Col du Crêt, from where one may traverse nearly horizontally under the Col des Chamois to the opening below the Col de Severeu (3111m.) at 2900m. Climb this wide opening over snow and rubble to the col ($1\frac{1}{2}$ h.). Now go up the S ridge of the mtn. on broken rock and snow, quite narrow, to an intermediate top (3241m.), descend to a little snow col (3196m.) at the head of the Mourti gl., and continue on the crest over steep rock to a shoulder/saddle (snow), then up a fairly steep mixed section to the summit ($1\frac{3}{4}$ h., $3\frac{1}{4}$ h. from Pantalons Blancs biv. hut).

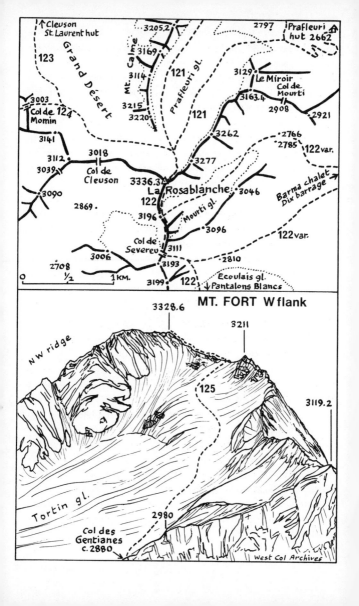

↑ Cleuson
St. Laurent hut

Grand Désert

3205.2
Mt. Calme
3169
3114
3215
3220

121 Prafleuri gl.
121

2797
Prafleuri hut 2662

3129
Le Miroir
Col de Mourti
3163.4
2908
2921

123

3003
Col de 124
Momin

3141
3112
3018
3039
Col de Cleuson
3090
2869.

3262
3277
2766
2785
122 var.

3336.3
La Rosablanche
122
3046
Barma chalet
Dix barrage

3196
Mourti gl.
Col de Severeu
3111
3096
122 var.

3006
2708
3193
2810

0   ½   1 KM.

3199   122

Ecoulais gl.
↓ Pantalons Blancs

MT. FORT W flank

3328.6
3211

NW ridge

125

3119.2

Tortin gl.

2980

Col des
Gentianes
c. 2880

West Col Archives

From North (Grand Désert/Cleuson). The most frequented approach on ski. Easy terrain all the way, the gl. becomes crevassed after mid season. F.

123 From the St. Laurent hut follow a good zigzag track SW then SE to the Lac de Cleuson (2642m.). Pass along W side of lake into the moraine cwm further S, giving access to the lower snow tongue of the Grand Désert gl. Go up moderate snow slopes due S then in a curve SE passing in turn some 300m. distance from the Col de Momin and Col de Cleuson on your R (crevasses). By keeping L pass near the base of the S rock ridge of Petit Mt. Calme, then trend R to join the NE ridge of the mtn. as for Rte. 121 ($3\frac{1}{4}$ h. from hut, $2\frac{1}{4}$ h. in descent).

From North-West (Fort). The longest approach to the mtn., nevertheless frequented from the popular Fort hut by mtn. scramblers. F.

124 From the Mt. Fort hut go up a track NW behind the hut, passing the junction with trail coming from the cableway. In a few min. the track turns ESE and crosses to moraine below the little Chaux gl. The track can be followed to the tarn at pt. 2709m. Continue up the L (N) side of the little gl. (snow) to the scree saddle of the Col de la Chaux (2940m.) ($1\frac{1}{2}$ h.). On the other side descend direct for 25m., then bear L (NE) on snow under a rockband and pass a tiny snow lake to reach scree/moraine which is crossed E into the hollow containing the Lac du Petit Mt. Fort (2764m.). Go round the L (NE) side of this lake and cross scree under a bluff on your L. In the same SSE direction follow up a scree/rock trench between rock bluffs towards pt. 2959m. on the Rochers de Momin ridge ahead. Below this bear L (E) into the bed of a hollow under the W side of the Col de Momin (3003m.). Ascend directly to this flattish opening, on the other E side level with the Grand Désert gl. ($1\frac{1}{2}$ h.). So join Rte. 123 which is followed to the summit ($1\frac{1}{2}$ h., $4\frac{1}{2}$ h. from Mt. Fort hut, $3\frac{3}{4}$ h. in descent).

MONT FORT 3328.6m.

LK 1326. Obviously named, this mtn. forms the last note-worthy summit at the N end of the Pleureur chain. Ascended by many rtes., none of them of special interest to the technical climber. However, a very popular excursion. Almost bereft of information in English literature. First recorded tourist ascent: E. Hoffmann-Burkhardt with S. Bessard, J. Fellay, 11 July, 1866.

<u>West Flank (from Col des Gentianes)</u>. The normal rte. from the Mt. Fort hut, pleasant, F+.

125 From the Mt. Fort hut follow Rte. 124 to the tarn at pt. 2709m. Turn L (N) and cross grass and stones, soon bearing R (NE) up a steep grass then rock slope to the saddle of the Col des Gentianes (c. 2880m.). Traces of a path on slopes further L ($1\frac{1}{4}$ h.). On the other side walk out on to the Tortin gl. and ascend its R (S) side, crevasses, towards a shoulder under the SW summit ridge, midway between the summit (L) and pt. 3211m. (R). Cross a small bergschrund and go up a fairly steep snow slope to this shoulder, then continue up the rocky ridge to the top ($1\frac{3}{4}$ h., 3 h. from hut; $1\frac{1}{2}$ h. in descent).

Note: The Tortin gl. can be joined from the bottom by starting from the roadhead at Tortin hamlet cableway sta. (2045m.), carparking, in the Val de Nendaz. From here, $3\frac{1}{2}$ h. to summit.

<u>South-East Ridge (from Col du Petit Mt. Fort)</u>. The easiest but not the most direct way on the E side. F+.

126 From the St. Laurent hut follow a good zigzag track SW then SE to the Lac de Cleuson (2642m.). Pass along W side of lake to the stream coming down from the Petit Mt. Fort gl. to the little tarn at pt. 2644m., some 150m. beyond S end of lake. Go up the R (N) side of this stream to the narrows giving access to the easy snow slopes of the gl. Climb these directly to the Col du Petit Mt. Fort saddle (3026m.), marked but not named on map, at the top (2 h.). Follow the saddle to a large snow/scree gully on R (E) side of ridge. Take this to a scree shoulder higher up. Where the ridge steepens again at the top of the shoulder, trend R over broken shelves on E side of crest, so turning a little tower, and rejoin crest at foot of summit riser. Climb this direct to top (45 min., $2\frac{3}{4}$ h. from hut; $1\frac{3}{4}$ h. in descent).

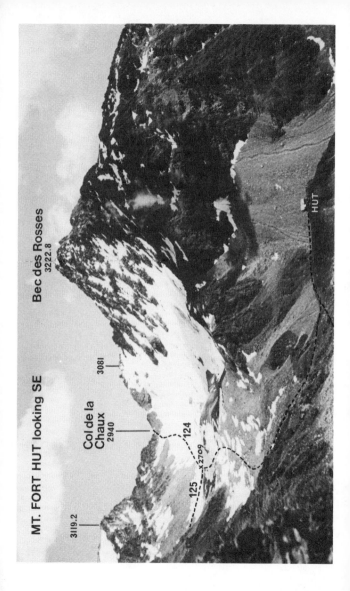

MT. FORT HUT looking SE

Bec des Rosses
3222.8

3119.2

Col de la
Chaux
2940

3081

125

2709

124

HUT

FRONTIER CHAIN

Mountain bases

Aiguillette Bivouac   3180m.

LK 1346. SAC. Not shown on map, situated on the rock island
called L'Aiguillette (3198.7m.) between its summit and snow
saddle to the immediate S, under the Bec de la Sasse and above
the Otemma gl. Opened in 1970, door unlocked, no warden,
14 places, cooking utensils, etc., take your own stove.

127 From the Chanrion hut follow Rte. 7 up the Otemma gl. to
2820m. Move to the R (S) side and go up the crevassed slope
just R of pt. 2937m. on to the Aiguillette gl. Ascend below
the rock island, reach the saddle at its inner (S) end, and the
hut (fixed cables) a few m. above ($3\frac{1}{4}$ h. from Chanrion hut).

128 From the Vignettes hut reverse Rte. 7 to same place on
Otemma gl. and so reach hut ($2\frac{3}{4}$ h.). Alternatively and slightly
more direct, from the Otemma gl. enter the Blanchen gl. bay
on N side of L'Aiguillette, keeping L below the Singla ridge to
near pt. 3092m., then make a slightly rising traverse across
the gl., crevasses in same direction, to the saddle behind
L'Aiguillette.

Sassa Bivouac   2973m.

LK 1346, 1366. Bivacco della Sassa. CAAI. Very old, original style Ital. biv. hut, door open, 4 places, cooking utensils,
take your own stove. Situated on a small rock shoulder at the
top of the lateral moraine near the bottom of the small Sassa
gl.

129 Start at the ruined site of Chamen (1715m.) on main road
in the Valpelline. In 1974 signs of rebuilding were evident

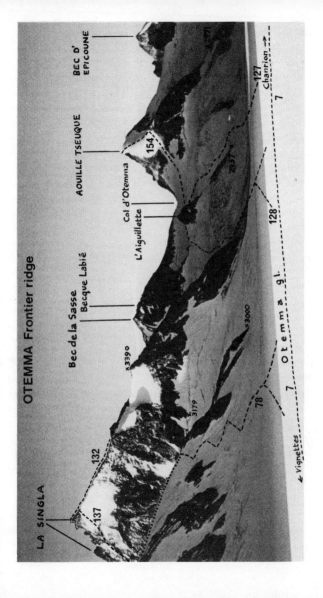

OTEMMA Frontier ridge

LA SINGLA

137   132

Bec de la Sasse

Becque Labië

×3390

3179

×3000

Col d'Otemma

L'Aiguillette

AOUILLE TSEUQUE

154

BEC D'
EPICOUNE

127
← Chanrion →
7

7237

128

7   Otemma gl.

78

← Vignettes

here. Carparking, signpost, old red waymarks. Follow a good track in zigzags to the Grand Chamen chalets (2018m.), beyond which the track contours towards the Sassa stream which is crossed L by a small bridge. On the other side cross grassy slopes to the Crotta chalet (2188m.). The now vague track circles R to recross the main stream (plank bridge) and follows the R side among blocks to another crossing place L (2288m.). The poor track now follows the stream into the Sassa cwm, crossing and re-crossing the stream twice before reaching a little rubble plain beside pt. 2528m. Ignore a track going L (N) towards a grassy bluff. Keep close to L side of the stream, waymarks on L, and follow moraine banks with large blocks to the long lateral moraine crest which leads at the top to snow patches. Cross L below rocks and return R to the shoulder and hut ($3\frac{1}{2}$-4 h. from road).

Spataro Bivouac   2600m.

LK 1366. Bivacco Franco Spataro. CAI. Not marked on map, situated just below top of a rock promontory (2615m.), on its NE side, in the Crête Sèche cwm. New in 1968, door open, 9 places, basic equipment and cooking utensils, take your own stove, water 50m. distant.

130 From Dzovenno (1575m.) in Valpelline follow a new road on N side in zigzags to Ruz hamlet (1696m.), limited carparking, 20 min. on foot. At the upper end of hamlet a path goes off L and zigzags generally N in woods to join a traverse path coming from L. Continue R (NE) across the Crête Sèche stream just above Casa Primo (1853m.). The path makes a long movement R through pleasant forest to join an open pasture where the Berrie (Berrier) chalets (2192m.) are found. Before the chalets turn back L (W) where another path traverses for over one km. to the Crête Sèche stream. As you approach the last hillock (2379m.) before reaching the stream, climb a grassy hump (track) to this pt. and continue at a similar distance from the Crête Sèche stream along a little spur rising N behind the hillock. Soon trend L, track mostly faint, above the rocky stream bank, and so reach the stream at 2500m., at the foot of a gorge and cliffs supporting promontory 2615m. Climb diagonally R to turn this side of the gorge and return L along the top, possibly snow, to the lower edge of the stream plain above. Cross the stream and bear round L (SW) to reach hut (about 3 h. from Dzovenno main road in Valpelline).

Regondi Bivouac   2590m.

LK 1366. Bivacco Nino Regondi. CAI. Neither marked nor named on map. Situated 50m. N of the Lago di Leitou (2538m.), upon a knoll in a commanding position on a rim of rocks running along the E side of the immense By cwm, thus directly below the WNW ridge of Mt. Clapier (Morion group). Door open, 6 places, fully equipped, cooking utensils, etc., take your own stove.

131 From the roadhead called Glacier (1549m.), about 3 km. above Ollomont village (bus service), cross the main river bridge below a ravine rising E. Ascend a steep track on R side of the ravine stream and after 40m. bear R along a vague track to a chalet at 1592m. Go up 20m. into the woods behind this chalet to join a good path coming up from the R. Follow it L to near the ravine stream, then climb in numerous zigzags steeply on R side of ravine to a crossing pt. fairly high up. The path continues looping L then R and finally twists up the ravine bed to a grassy hollow. At the top of this bear R up grassy slopes to Le Piazze chalets (2149m.), then contour slopes E and reach the flat ground of the Piano del Breuil. Contour round S side of this plain, crossing a tributary stream, for about 500m. distance to where a small but good track climbs the slope above, to the S. Go up this with several zigzags in the top part to the rim of a basin behind, where the Lago dell'Incliousa is situated. The track turns L (NE) and passes just below rocky hummocks, then over a grassy hillock to the N edge of the Lago di Leitou. The hut is found on a knoll just to N again (3 h. from Glacier roadhead).

Note: The approach from Ollomont village over the Colle Cornet is steep, tiresome and partly trackless (4 h.).

Otemma-Valpelline North Chain

This chain marks the Swiss-Ital. frontier down to Mt. Gelé and the Fenêtre de Durand, from where the Morion sub-chain is detached on the Ital. side. One of the most varied, interesting but least known parts of the Pennine Alps. One biv. hut on the Swiss side, the remaining similar huts are on the Ital. side (see above). Otemma = Hautemma = highest pasture.

COL D'OREN   3262m.

LK 1346, 1347. Between the Ptes. d'Oren and La Singla, an old gl. pass from the Otemma gl. to the head of the Valpelline. Though claimed as a variation of the High Level Route, it has hardly ever been used for this expedition and today is certainly not recommended. See Rtes. 135, 136. First tourist crossing: C. H. & W. F. Fox, F. F. Tuckett with J. J. Bennen, P. Perren, 26 June, 1861.

LA SINGLA   3714.1m.

LK 1346, 1347. Ital: La Sengla, or Cengla = the girdle or steep ledged band, comparable with Cengalo/Bregaglia. A long roof-like rock massif with a unique saw tooth crest running N-S between Col d'Oren (3262m.) and the Col E de Blanchen (c. 3560m.). The ridge is about 2 km. long (1500m. on the main crest) and as a traverse it provides one of the finest expeditions of its kind in the Pennine Alps.

The ridge is marked by three main summits: Singla N (3714.1m.), Singla Central (3704m.), Singla S (3691m., 3690m. IGM). Beyond this the S end proper is marked by the Grand Blanchen (q. v.). Beyond the N summit the ridge divides; a NE branch descends to Col d'Oren, a NW branch to the Otemma gl. The latter spur provides the usual approach and descent on the Swiss side. The N summit is distinctly harder to reach from the Ital. side.

Climbing history. First ascent N Peak: C. Schroeder with S. Bessard, 22 July, 1867. On the same day a companion climbed the Central Peak solo: A. Baltzer. Both ascents were made by the W face, Baltzer forking R to reach the lowest gap between the N and Central tops, the other pair forking L to attain the N peak. A curious affair arising from a disagreement on the mtn. First ascent S Peak: E. Canzio, F. Mondini with G. Noro, 18 August, 1898, by its E spur.

<u>North Peak by West Flank and North-West Ridge</u>. The most frequented rte. to recent times but the least direct. In the fall line of the N Peak a rock rib (Chasseron Spur) descends to the gl. at pt. 3092m. This rib divides two fairly large hanging snowfields on the W face. The rte. makes a rising traverse across the L-hand (N) snowfield to the ridge. Mixed climbing, interesting, AD with pitches of II+. Some stonefall danger. Most of the rte. was climbed by F. Hoffmann-Merian with B. & J. Fellay, 8 July, 1867, who retreated from near the top in a storm and just failed to make the first ascent.

132 From the Aiguillette biv. make a slightly descending traverse across the lower snow terrace of the Blanchen gl., crevasses in same direction, to the foot of the abovementioned rib. Either climb a steep snow/ice couloir (bergschrund) on the immediate L of rib, or 60m. further L take steep rocks and snow patches, to reach the hanging snowfield above. Work diagonally L across the snow, below a bergschrund, and so reach the NW spur of the mtn. Follow the rock crest on pleasantly exposed slabs to a snowhead and junction with the main frontier ridge at c. 3660m. After a short horizontal section, turn a gendarme on the L, sometimes icy slabs, then follow the main crest on splendid slabs with several small pinnacles to the N peak ($2\frac{1}{2}$-3 h. from Aiguillette biv.).

133 Variation by the W rock rib, base pt. 3092m., called the Chasseron Spur. See above. Enter the couloir of the usual rte. and almost immediately move R to climb rocks up the side of this rib to its crest. Follow the crest with pitches of II/II+ to the steeper upper section which gives several short pitches of III and finishes precisely at the summit. Snow/ice

146

on the rib makes the climbing much harder (2 h. from foot of couloir). J. M. Béguelin, J. C. Berthoud, J. Page, M. Tombey, R. Marcoz, 13 August, 1972.

<u>North Peak by West Flank Original Route</u>. See preamble to Rte. 132. This line follows the R-hand (S) hanging snowfield. Quite direct, mixed terrain with loose rock in upper section. Some stonefall danger. PD/PD+. First ascensionists.

134 From the Aiguillette biv., as for Rte. 132 to below the W flank. On the R side of the W rib (pt. 3092m.) climb through a loose rock/ice gutter to reach the snowfield and go up this near its centre to a bergschrund below rocks funnelling up to the lowest gap in the main ridge between the N (L) and Central (R) peaks. Above the bergschrund follow ribs and gullies just L of the line below the gap. Some 50m. below the gap slant L under the main ridge to work across ledges and slabs rising L to join the ridge in a gap between the N forepeak and the N peak proper. Continue along the main ridge briefly to the top ($2\frac{1}{2}$-3 h. from Aiguillette biv.).

<u>North-East (Frontier) Ridge (from Col d'Oren)</u>. This jagged ridge is a more serious proposition than the previous rtes. and is generally started from the Vignettes hut. It is the most direct way to reach the N peak from the Ital. side and is preferable to the stone bombarded ribs on the E flank of the mtn. Unfavourable conditions make the climbing delicate and unpleasant. Average angle, 40°. AD+ in good conditions (rare), pitches of III. First ascent: A. S. Jenkins with J. Bournissen, J. Gaudin, 27 June, 1911.

135 From the Vignettes hut follow the usual trail over the Col de Chermotane and descend the Otemma gl. to the foot of the Petit Mt. Collon gl. branch on your L. Go up in the centre SSE then continue somewhat R towards Col d'Oren, cross a bergschrund and finish up a short snow/ice slope and rocks (3262m.). F/F+ (2 h. from Vignettes hut).

136 From the Col Collon hut follow a faint traverse path W in grass and stones for some distance, until this line passes below a rock barrier whose base is at the same level as the hut. This barrier slants down to the L. Near its lowest L-hand pt. it is cut by a rock/grass couloir. Climb this couloir, exiting L at the top, to attain a moraine field running up to the Oren Nord gl. Ascend rubble trending slightly L, and cross a low rockband to reach the gl. Go up this directly towards Col d'Oren, finishing up a short gully. F/F+ (2 h. from Col Collon hut).

137 From Col d'Oren follow a steepening crest on rotten rock, turning short obstacles to L or R, up to a small snowy shoulder. The next steep section is best taken slightly L of the crest on mixed terrain, awkward, to rejoin the ridge at the foot of a continuously steep snow crest. Climb a rock fringe marking the L side of the snow crest, then make a direct ascent of a snow/ice slope to a level bit of ridge just beyond the snowhead at top of the NW spur. So join Rte. 132 which is followed to summit (3-4 h. from col, 5-6 h. from Vignettes or Col Collon huts).

GRAND BLANCHEN   3678.7m.   3680m. IGM

LK 1346, 1347. Ital: Gran Becca Blanchen. The gable S end of the Singla ridge. Seen end on from the S it presents a triangular rock facet. From the apex of this facet the first 80m. of the Singla ridge is followed to reach the highest pt. proper of the Blanchen. Probably the most popular excursion for parties at the Aiguillette biv. hut. An easy climb from the Sassa biv. and one of the relatively frequented summits of the Valpelline North area, being an excellent viewpoint. "The beauty of the view ... I had rarely been so charmed with a mountain prospect" (Cust). First ascent: A. Cust with P.
148

Beytrison, J. Martin, 23 September, 1879.

<u>South-West (Frontier) Ridge (from Col E de Blanchen)</u>. Almost all ascents are made by this rte., an excellent outing, highly recommended. F+ with little rock pitches of II-. Crevassed gl. terrain on Swiss side. The col (c. 3560m.) is neither marked nor named on map. It is exactly where grid line 87 crosses the ridge. First ascensionists.

138 From the Aiguillette biv. hut descend S from the rock island, cross the Blanchen gl. plateau E towards the flank of the Singla ridge, then bear SE over a bergschrund and climb the broken upper gl. slopes cut by crevasses and in parts fairly steep to a final bergschrund and the col (1 h.). In the right conditions, long glissades are possible in descent.

139 From the Sassa biv. hut follow a faint track over rubble, then snow, NE, keeping L above a large rockband cutting the small Sassa gl., until you can join the upper and steeper snowfield of this gl. coming down from the Colle della Sassa (3256m.). Go up the gl. to just below the col, then bear L (N) and continue up fairly steep snow and rubble below the S facet of the mtn. on your R. So reach a short, loose rockband under the col which is mounted to the foot of the ridge ($1\frac{3}{4}$ h.).

140 From the Col E de Blanchen follow the generally easy sharp rock crest with several large blocks, turned by short flanking movements L, to a shoulder marking the top of the S facet. Continue along the main ridge, avoiding two small towers on the L side to reach the highest pt. (45 min., $1\frac{3}{4}$ h. from Aiguillette biv., $2\frac{1}{2}$ h. from Sassa biv.).

141 Simple traverse. This is more convenient from the Swiss side, but can be followed from the Ital. side by returning over the Col E de Blanchen. PD+. From the summit continue along

149

the main Singla ridge to N, now much narrower and with fine, exposed situations. Traverse or turn on the L side five small towers with nice slabby pitches and some loose rock (II/II+) to reach in 170m. distance a gap marking the lowest pt. in ridge between the Blanchen and Singla S Peak. From here descend the W side, down rocks leading into a steep snow couloir. Take this and go over a bergschrund to reach a gl. bay adjoining the main part of the Blanchen gl. Keep L then R and descend across the gl. to rejoin the lower part of Rte. 138. So reach the Aiguillette biv. in a few min. ($1\frac{1}{2}$ h. from summit to biv. hut).

<u>Singla Traverse</u>. See preambles to La Singla and Grand Blanchen, above. A magnificent high level expedition, much less convenient when starting from an Ital. base because the descent rtes. involve reascents in crossing passes to regain the starting pt. The best base is the Aiguillette biv., for the traverse in either direction. The pros and cons of traversing N-S or S-N are described separately. Either way this is a long and difficult climb with a character of its own. Longer and more serious than the Aigs. Rouges. Comparable with the Bouquetins, though more sustained on the whole while less exacting at the crux pitches. The ridge carries 30 to 35 gendarmes, peaklets or summits. There are no extreme pitches and the hardest ones are well protected. Most parties have traversed S-N, but the best way seems to be N-S. One of the most attractive and least known expeditions of its class in the Pennine Alps.

First complete traverse S-N: M. Gilbert with J. Follonier, A. Georges, 15 August, 1926. Second: A. S. Jenkins with guides, 20 August, 1927. First N-S: G. V. Amoretti with C. Grivel, 9-10 August, 1937. Both parties making these first traverses avoided most of the true crest between the N and Central Peaks by unpleasant movements on the W side. First traverses of crest throughout, S-N: H. Mercier, E. Pidoux, 18 August, 1953. An elderly English couple with a guide (Gaudin) followed this party. N-S: H. Mercier, P. Metzker, E. Pidoux, 27 July, 1960. First winter traverse from N to S Peaks, excluding the Blanchen: R. Willy with M. Siegenthaler, 3 January, 1975.

<u>South-North Traverse.</u> In this direction the two key pitches are climbed, whereas in the other direction they are descended by abseiling. Working S-N, it is possible to avoid abseils, although a double rope will prove useful in two or three places. The key pitches are situated in the last part of the section between the S and Central summits. One of them can be turned, but not to much advantage. In this direction the climbing is more sustained and interesting, but there are long descent sections on rounded slabs which are too steep to tackle facing outwards, yet not steep enough to warrant facing inwards. You have to move in an awkward half-crouching position which is clumsy and tiring. In the N-S (opposite) direction these scaly, overlapping slabs give pleasant rapid climbing. D overall, continuous pitches of III, some of IV and two of IV+. Rock good on the whole but there are loose parts.

142 From the Aiguillette biv. take Rtes. 138, 140 to the top of the Grand Blanchen, and continue by Rte. 141 into the lowest gap between the Blanchen and S Peak ($2\frac{1}{4}$ h.). From here traverse several larger gendarmes; first there is a needle like pinnacle of greenish rock, about 18m. high. Next a high tower with two prongs, from where the prominent E spur of the mtn. is detached. Turn this tower either on the L (Swiss) side by rotten rock, with a couloir to finish; or on the R, across the top of the spur, preferable; the latter may be impossible due to a large cornice. Either way reach the gap behind the tower. Ahead are three pointed gendarmes; traverse the first by the exposed crest, and continue to the top of the second, which is a large exposed flake. Start down this by lowering over a smooth vertical wall on the R (Ital.) side (3m., IV+), followed

151

GD. EPICOUNE 3346 156
Col 3259 155
3461
Aouille Tseuque 3535 154
3554
Col d' Otemma 3209 153
Becque Labie 3463 152
Bec de la Sasse 3496 150
Pte. de Boette 3541 147
Petit Blanchen Col W 144 146
Col E 139

GD. CHAMEN

B. CHATELE

B. BOVET

Morio chain

L' Evêque

Mt. Collon

Bouquetins

ecca
es Lacs
3470
143

Ptes.
d'Oren
77

Mitre

Col Collon

Pte.
Kurz
3498.3

n

L. MORT

OREN

Mt. Gelé
3518.2
163~4

Gd. Combin

Chardoney
3447
160

Cervo
3441
159

Bec d'
Epicoune

nodo
3528.8
157

Bca.
Picion
3393

Col
3233

Gd.
Epicoune
3346
156

VERT TZAN

TOUR DE LA TSA

GD. CHAMEN

by 10m. of delicate climbing to rejoin the crest which leads into a deep gap. From here climb L in a spiralling movement and rejoin the crest at the top of the step above the gap. Follow the jagged crest to Singla S ($1\frac{3}{4}$ h.).

The next section to Singla Central has very steep flanks and is cut by two deep gaps. There are a dozen or so gendarmes. First, descend two slabby steps which are separated by a gendarme, with a horizontal knife edge. Continue down over two fine gendarmes to a final slab section (25m.) leading into the first deep gap. Above is a vertical 12m. step. Climb this direct, delicate, doubtful rock, IV/IV+. Continue over three smaller gendarmes to where the crest forms a large knoll, Le Crâne. This can be climbed direct, with a slight overhang to finish, IV, cairn on top, and descended on the far side by a short abseil. However, it is turned more easily on the R (Ital.) side. Return to the crest and descend another series of steep slabs into the second deep gap. From the gap make a rising traverse R for a few m. on poor rock to a dièdre of loose yellow rock. Climb this, 12m., IV+, to the crest. Continue to a spear-like gendarme which is turned on the L. Several more rope lengths lead to a large scree terrace at the foot of the step below the Central summit. Climb the broad easy crest for 15m. to a vertical red wall with a conspicuous crack. Climb the crack, 15m., IV+, to a large peg at the top (2 h.).

This final wall can be avoided by a long flanking movement on the L (Swiss) side. This starts about 35m. below the summit, before you reach the final wall. Cross the W flank on very steep rock (dièdres and slabby walls, IV) and rejoin the crest beyond (N of) Singla Central.

From the Central summit to Singla N you have the longest section of the ridge. First descend on the crest by another series of slabs and gendarmes with compact rock. Traverse everything until you reach the last gendarme, which is square-topped. Turn this on the R (Ital.) side. Continue down another series of steep slabs, exposed but with good holds, into a deep gap. The last pitch into the gap is particularly steep (over-hanging on crest), and an abseil is useful. The landing in the gap can be delicate on account of snow. The step above is 12m. high. Climb this by the vertical crest, IV, exposed, and continue more easily to a forepeak. There follows 200m. of pleasant crest, over small towers and gaps, to the true N Peak ($2\frac{1}{2}$ h., $6\frac{3}{4}$ h. from Grand Blanchen, $8\frac{1}{2}$ h. from Aiguillette biv., halts excluded).

From Singla N descend preferably by Rte. 132 to the Aig-uillette biv. (2 h., $10\frac{1}{2}$ h., normally 13-15 h. including halts).

<u>North-South Traverse.</u> This seems to be the best way. As indicated above, you abseil down the key IV+ pitches (easily arranged), and the long slab sections are quite pleasant in ascent; the rock here is usually excellent. D, fairly sus-tained, numerous pitches of IV.

142A From the Aiguillette biv. ascend to the N Peak by Rtes. 132 or 133 ($2\frac{1}{2}$ h.). From the N Peak follow the crest to the N forepeak, then descend a long section to the lowest gap. There is a final pitch of 12m. on the crest to reach the gap (IV, or abseil). The gap may be a fine snow crest. Climb out of it by a slightly overhanging pitch, IV, shoulder useful, and con-tinue up steep slabs with good holds to below a square-shaped gendarme, which is turned on the L (Ital.) side. Now follow the crest to the Central Peak.

From a large peg in place, abseil 15m. down the first step to a terrace. Continue down the ridge, turning a spear-shaped gendarme on the R. Reach the top of a step above the first deep gap in this section. (In the reverse direction this is where you climb the loose dièdre somewhat on the Ital. side). Abseil 15m. into the gap. Above is the Crâne. Either traverse it by the crest (IV), or turn on the L side with comparative ease.

155

LA SINGLA E side

142 →

← 137

A B C D E F GH J K L M N P S S S

Comba d'Oren

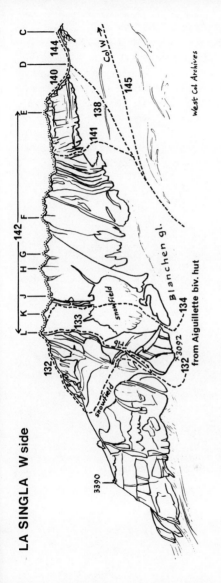

LA SINGLA W side

from Aiguillette biv. hut

Blanchen gl.

snowfield

snowfield

West Col Archives

A Becca des Lacs 3470m.
B Colle della Sassa 3256m.
C Petit Blanchen 3592m.
D Col E de Blanchen c. 3560m.
E Grand Blanchen 3678.7m.
F Singla S 3691m.
G Le Crâne 3704m.
H Singla Central 3704m.

J square-topped gendarme
K Singla N forepeak
L Singla N 3714.1m.
M Col d'Oren 3262m.
N Gran Vanna 3301m.
P Becca Vannetta 3361m.
S Pres. d' Oren 3525m.

Traverse the next gendarmes, then descend into the second deep gap; this is reached by a vertical step of doubtful rock (IV/IV+, or abseil). Climb out of the gap by typical slab pitches, traverse several gendarmes and reach the top of Singla S.

The rte. from Singla S to the Blanchen is identical as for traversing in the opposite direction. There is a short bit of IV+ (3m.) and several bits of IV (from N Peak to Le Blanchen, (7 h.).

Descend as for Rtes. 140, 138 in reverse to the Aiguillette biv. (about 11 h. for round trip excluding halts).

BECCA DES LACS   3470m.

143 LK 1346, 1347.   The highest pt. of the "Lakes Group" of summits, a subsidiary massif in two large rock wings overlooking the Place Moulin barrage in Valpelline. Fine regional view.   Easily climbed by the NW ridge from the Colle della Sassa (3256m., 3259m. IGM), Rte. 139, in 2 h. from the Sassa biv.   First ascent: E. Canzio, F. Mondini with G. Noro, 28 August, 1897.

COL E DE BLANCHEN   c. 3560m.

LK 1346, 1347.   Neither marked nor named on map, situated at the foot of the SW frontier ridge of the Grand Blanchen.   See Rtes. 138, 139.   First traverse: A. Cust with P. Beytrison, J. Martin, 23 September, 1879.

PETIT BLANCHEN   3592m.   3591m. IGM

144 LK 1346, 1347.   Little rock summit only a few min. scramble along ridge from the Col E de Blanchen, Rtes. 138, 139. Fine viewpoint. First ascent as for Col E and the Grand Blanchen.

COL COLLON HUT looking SW

Gd Blanchen

AIG.
ROUGES
3460

Becca
des Lacs
3470

Col des
Lacs

COLLE DELLA
SASSA
3256

143

289

COL W DE BLANCHEN   c. 3475m.

LK 1346, 1347.   Neither marked nor named on map.   A relatively deep depression in the frontier ridge between the Petit
Blanchen and Pte. de Boette, the easiest pass across this part
of the frontier chain, with a new importance in making a short
link between the Aiguillette and Sassa biv. huts.   Both sides,
F/F+.   First traverse: A. Cust, J.B. Parish with J. Maître,
25 August, 1881.

145 Swiss (N) side.   From the Aiguillette biv. follow Rte. 138
as for the Col E.   From the lower part of the steeper upper
crevassed slopes of the Blanchen gl. trend R towards the foot
of the obvious snow saddle of the col.   Cross a bergschrund,
or if wide turn on R, and climb a short snow/ice slope to the
top ($1\frac{1}{4}$ h.).

146 Ital. (S) side.   From the Sassa biv. climb N up a scree
spur to rubble and snowfields under the pass.   Continue direct
into a steep couloir.   If this has good snow follow it to top,
otherwise use easy rocks on L side ($1\frac{1}{2}$ h.).

POINTE DE BOETTE   3541m.

147 LK 1346.   Ital: Punta Boetta.   Simple ridge summit of no
special interest, easily climbed from the Col W de Blanchen
by the SE frontier ridge in 30 min.   First ascent: as for Col
W de Blanchen.

BEC DE LA SASSE   3496m.   3497m. IGM

LK 1346.   Ital: Becca della Sassa.   This summit rises directly
behind the Aiguillette biv. hut and offers some rock climbing
interest.   First ascent: A. Cust with P. Georges, P. Maître,
26 July, 1897.

<u>North Ridge.</u>   A short rock climb on excellent granite in the
upper part.   AD with pitches of III.   First ascent: J.L. & M.

Blanc, 31 July, 1956.

148 From the Aiguillette biv. work up L under the ridge on the Blanchen gl. side, passing below a large gendarme marking the bottom of the ridge. Now bear R, cross a bergschrund and climb a couloir L of the gendarme (stonefall) to the ridge. Go up this fairly easily to a large yellow tower. Turn this L over a series of ledges and rejoin the ridge behind by climbing short walls divided by gritty ledges. Continue on the upper ridge by the crest with a series of fine pitches of moderate difficulty to the top (3 h. from biv. hut).

149 Descent. The shortest way down is to follow the easy E (frontier) ridge to the Col de Boette, neither marked nor named on map, c. 3450m. (15 min.). Descend the N side down a steep snow/ice slope of 100m. with outcrops (abseils if required), and cross a double bergschrund, can be difficult, into a bay of the Blanchen gl. Go down this with crevasses to the biv. hut below. PD/PD+ $(1\frac{1}{2}$ h.).

150 A longer but easier descent. From the summit follow the main frontier ridge S to the Becque Labié (3463m.) (q. v.), then descend its W ridge to the broad Col d'Otemma (3209m.), and from here by gentle snowfields across the Aiguillette gl. to the biv. hut (2 h.). Alternatively, halfway along the frontier ridge towards the Becque Labié, descend an obvious steep snow couloir with a bergschrund to the gl. below (first ascensionists' rte.). F+/PD.

West Face Buttress. The buttress flanks the L side of the couloir mentioned in the alternative for Rte. 150, which cuts the middle of the rock wall contained between the Sasse and Labié. Good rock, a few pegs and one wedge used. Several pitches of IV/IV+ and one of A1, sustained in top section. 300m. First ascent: G. Singer, F. Trèves with R. Marcoz,

25 August, 1972.

151 From the Aiguillette biv. reach the foot of the couloir across the easy Aiguillette gl. in 30 min. Cross the bergschrund and climb the couloir for a few m. to the first rocks on L. Traverse L and climb grey slabs direct to a wall. Turn this on the R and continue up slabs on the crest line to a red wall. Take this direct (IV+) followed by another grey wall pitch (IV, peg) to more slabs. Near the top of the slabs keep a little R and go up a loose chimney (III) to a small shoulder. Above this climb rocks to the foot of an overhanging gendarme. Take this direct by a vague groove (A1, then IV, 2 pegs, wedge) to a good stance 10m. above the hard bit. Continue up a sharp exposed ridge (IV/IV+) to the top of a gendarme. Abseil 8m. to the gap below and continue up the crest (IV) to a rockhead, taken direct (move of IV+). From the top of this abseil 15m. to the L (N) down a wall, then scramble up rock to join the main frontier ridge (3-4 h. from bergschrund). For descent, see Rtes. 149, 150.

BECQUE (BECCA) LABIÉ   3463m.   3462m. IGM

152 LK 1346. Above Col d'Otemma, secondary summit forming
S end of a rock roof whose N end is the Bec de la Sasse. No
special interest, easily climbed by its W (frontier) ridge from
Col d'Otemma in 45 min. , Rte. 150. First ascent: G.E. Foster
with H. Baumann, 7 August, 1866.

COL D'OTEMMA   3209m.   3211m. IGM

153 LK 1346. Between the Becque Labié and Aouille Tseuque,
a broad, easy snow saddle depression on the N (Swiss) side,
but having a crumbling rock wall on the other side, PD. Rarely
crossed. First tourist traverse: A. Cust with X. Andermatten, 21 August, 1882.

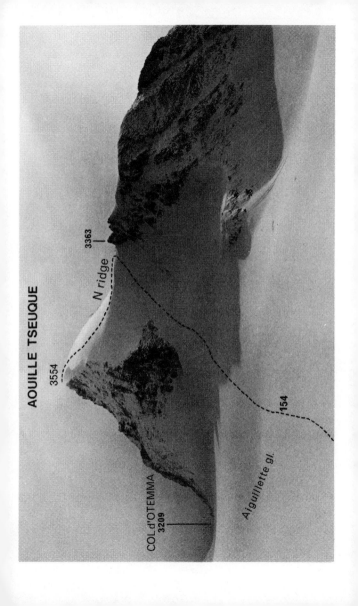

AOUILLE TSEUQUE

3554

N ridge

3363

COL d'OTEMMA
3209

154

Aiguillette gl.

AOUILLE TSEUQUE   3554m.

LK 1346, 1366. Ital: Aouille Tseucca = "Hornless" mtn. A
large hulk with multi tops whose extent is not readily appreci-
ated on the Swiss side. One of the more frequented summits
of the frontier ridge, but rarely climbed from the Ital. side.
After 1920 most ascents can be attributed to parties making a
detour from the High Level Route. The Aiguillette biv. now
provides a convenient base for an overnight halt and a short
worthwhile climb. Rpt. Roberts, 1975. First ascent: A. Baltzer, C. Schroeder with S. Bessard, 31 July, 1867.

North-North-East Ridge. The most obvious rte. on the Otemma
side, climbed more often than all other ways put together. A
simple snow climb with fine situations. F+. First ascensionists, in descent.

154 From the Aiguillette biv. cross the Aiguillette gl. SW and
move a little L to the foot of a fairly steep snow slope rising
up the side of the NNE ridge. Ascend this slope to a saddle
just beyond pt. 3363m., then follow the broad ridge to summit
($1\frac{3}{4}$ h. from biv. hut).

COL DE L'AOUILLE TSEUQUE   3259m.

155 LK 1366. Between the Aouille Tseuque and Grand Epicoune,
a moderately difficult pass of no special interest. First recorded traverse: M. Kurz with C. Favre, 15 October, 1922.

GRAND EPICOUN(E)   3346m.   3345m. IGM.

156 LK 1366. A small rock peak with generally sound granite,
seldom climbed. The SW frontier ridge has several tower
pts. before reaching the Col d'Epicoune, none of which are
marked or named on LK: Denti d'Epicoune (c. 3290m.) and
Pta. Maria Luisa (3317m. IGM). The SE spur of the former
offers a modern rock climb of 400m., V (G. & S. Buscaini,
G. & L. Rossi, 4 August, 1970). First ascent: E. Canzio,
F. Mondini, N. Vigna, 24 August, 1897.

COL D'EPICOUNE   3233m.   3243m. IGM

LK 1366.   A deep gap between the Gd. Epicoune and Becca
Picion.   Moderately difficult on Swiss side, never climbed on
Ital. side.

BECCA PICION   3393m.

LK 1366.   A secondary rock peak with some interesting but
remote rock climbing.   Good rock.   First recorded ascent:
Miss D. E. Pilley, I. A. Richards, 5 September, 1923.

BEC D'EPICOUNE   3528. 8m.   3529m. IGM

LK 1366. Ital. name, preferable for this quite individual summit, is Becca Rayette. This name appears as a subsidiary S
summit (3432m.) on LK, in itself more subsidiary than another
pt. further up the frontier ridge, at the junction of the SW and
S ridges, and called in Italy the Nodo della Rayette (3444m.
IGM).   The LK Becca Rayette (3432m.) is dismissed as La
Rayette by the Italians. Rayette = tiers of grassy ledges on a
steep face.   Prior to the construction of the Aiguillette biv.,
easily the most frequented mtn. in the Otemma-Valpelline frontier chain, often climbed from the Chanrion hut. The Ital. side
remains a long pull up from the Valpelline, although it can now
be done conveniently from the Spataro biv. hut.
   First ascent: J. J. Weilenmann with J. Gillioz, 21 July,
1866.   First British ascent: C. L. & T. G. Longstaff with J.
Maître, P. Maurys, 27 August, 1897, by SSW ridge from Ital.
side.

North Ridge. The usual Swiss rte., a fine scramble and snow
climb, recommended. PD.

157 From the Chanrion hut follow Rte. 7 as for the Col de Chermotane, as far as the lower edge of the Otemma gl. at c. 2600m.
At this pt. cross the gl. SE to bad rubble against the moraine
running up briefly to the SW corner of the Jardin des Chamois.
Go up rocks R of the moraine and climb the L side of the Epicoune gl. until a narrow bay opens to the L. Turn into this
and climb trending L to the ridge at the back which is reached

at a narrow col marked pt. 3191m. Further R, towards the ridge proper, is a lower ridge gap, pt. 3185m. of less easy access. Follow the rock ridge over or round several small towers with a short, steep descent into gap 3185m. (2¾ h.). Start up the N ridge on steep rock, turning two small towers on the R, then easing for a short way until it merges into a fine snow ridge. In icy conditions this can be slow and laborious, but with good snow it goes quickly and directly to the summit. Cornices possible (1-2 h., about 4½ h. on average from Chanrion hut).

Variation. Instead of turning L into the gl. bay, continue past its entrance and the broken rib enclosing it. At c. 3100m. climb snow R of the rib. A snow tongue funnels up at 40° through broken rocks and leads with a riblet on the R to the first part of the snow ridge proper. In good conditions, shorter and quicker than taking the ridge from pt. 3191m.

158 From the Spataro biv. in much the same time, by the Col du Chardoney (3185m.), Rte. 161, followed by a slightly descending then rising traverse across the top of the Epicoune gl. to join the variation of Rte. 157 (4½ h. to summit).

MONTE CERVO 3441m.

159 LK 1366. Pleasant conical rockhead on S side of Bec d'Epicoune, most easily climbed as a diversion after reaching the latter summit by the one km. long but easy N-S linking snow ridge with rock to finish, interesting (1½ h. each way). From the Ital.-Valpelline side by the Combe de Vert Tsan, 5½ h. First ascent: L. Kurz, H. Riekel with J. & J. Bessard, 14 August, 1892. Second ascent (British): A. G. Topham with J. Maître, P. Maurys, 20 July, 1894 (started from Arolla! Made first crossing of Col de la Rayette and reached summit same day after 13¾ h. walking).

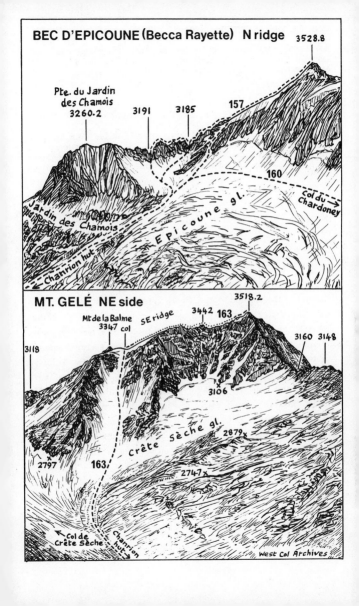

BEC D'EPICOUNE (Becca Rayette) N ridge

3528.8

Pte. du Jardin
des Chamois
3260.2

3191   3185   157

160

Col du
Chardoney →

Jardin des Chamois

E p i c o u n e   g l.

Chanrion hut

MT. GELÉ NE side   3518.2

Mt. de la Balme   SE ridge   3442   163
3347 col

3118   3160   3148

3106

crête sèche gl.   2879 x

2797   163   2747 x

← Col de
Crête Sèche

Chanrion
hut →

West Col Archives

COL DE LA RAYETTE   3320m.   3354m. IGM

LK 1366.   Between the Becca Rayette (Bec d'Epicoune) and
Bec du Chardoney, a fairly difficult pass (AD) on Swiss side,
easy on the Ital. First traverse as M. Cervo above.

BEC DU CHARDONEY   E. 3447m.   W. 3407m.

LK 1366. Ital: Becca Chardoney. An attractive mtn. of snow
and rock, and a fine viewpoint. Climbed not infrequently but
the Bec d'Epicoune has exercised more appeal at the Chardoney's expense. First ascent: A. Cust with X. Andermatten,
22 August, 1882.

West Flank and West-North-West Ridge. The usual rte. from
the Swiss side, variable, quite interesting and worthwhile,
PD/PD+.   Ridge climbed by E. Jenny with A. Burgener, E.
Crettez, 20 July, 1921.   Couloir descended by M. Kurz with
C. Favre, 17 October, 1922.

160 From the Chanrion hut follow Rtes. 7, 157 to the upper
plateau of the Epicoune gl. Cross this SW under the Epicoune
and Chardoney summits to the Col du Chardoney (3185m.)
($3\frac{1}{2}$ h.).   A shorter and quicker way up the Epicoune gl., following its W bank under the Tourme des Boucs ridge depends
on the state of crevasses on this side, but has been followed
often in early season.

From the Col du Chardoney either (a) climb the WSW ridge
direct on fairly good rock, making slight turning movements
at steep pitches, but otherwise following the crest with sustained climbing at II+, up to the W summit (3407m.) ($2\frac{1}{2}$ h.),
or (b), easier, shorter but exposed to stonefall; from the col
traverse horizontally SE on snow and rock below the WNW
ridge to the big, obvious couloir cutting the W flank for 200m.,
right up to pt. 3407m. Climb this steeply using the R branch
at 80m., on snow and easy rock (stonefall) to exit L on to the
WNW ridge about 25m. below pt. 3407m. ($1\frac{1}{2}$ h.).   From

168

pt. 3407m. go along the broad main ridge on snow (cornice on N side) and finally some rocks to the main E summit (15 min., $6\frac{1}{4}$ h. by ridge, $5\frac{1}{4}$ h. by couloir from Chanrion hut).

161 From the Spataro biv. hut to the Col du Chardoney, easy. Follow a little track N up a valley plain cut by several streams and bear L in the direction of the stream coming down from near pt. 2751m. Go up a rough slope to snowy/scree flats just L of this pt., then continue due N up a steep little cwm bed with tracks, under a large rockband R, to the Col de Crête Sèche (2899.1m.) (1 h.). Traverse R below the frontier ridge on your L, over stones and blocks to moraines which are crossed R to a nearly level spot in the upper Crête Sèche cwm. Ascend in the middle over snowbeds then either trend L to a lateral moraine, or follow snow in the middle, to the Col du Chardoney at the top (1 h., 2 h. from biv. hut). For the couloir in Rte. 160, bear R below the col ($3\frac{3}{4}$-$4\frac{3}{4}$ h. to summit from Spataro biv. according to rte.).

<u>South-West Ridge (from Col Berlon)</u>. The easiest and quickest way from the Spataro biv. hut. F+, short pitches of II.

162 From the Spataro biv., as for Rte. 161 to just below Col Berlon (3009m.), situated on your R in the upper Crête Sèche cwm. Reach the col in a few min. over rocks and snow ($1\frac{1}{4}$ h.). Now follow the ridge by its crest on good rock all the way, turning two or three steep pitches on the R side, to an upper loose section leading to shoulder pt. 3282m. Continue easily over broken rock and snow just R of crest to a short snow slope leading to the W summit (3407m.) (2 h.). Now along the easy main crest as for Rte. 160 to the main E summit (15 min., $3\frac{1}{2}$ h. from biv. hut).

COL DU CHARDONEY   3185m.   3186m. IGM

LK 1366.   Between the Bec du Chardoney and Tourme des Boucs, a gl. pass used mainly for access to the Chardoney and Bec d'Epicoune.   See Rtes. 160, 161.   First traverse: J. J. Weilenmann with J. Gillioz, 21 July, 1866.

COL DE CRÊTE SÈCHE   2899.1m.

LK 1366.   A smugglers' pass in the W side of the Crête Sèche cwm, barely distinguishable as a col, but known since the 16th century and frequented long before mtn. explorers came on the scene as an easy passage from Mauvoisin (Chanrion hut) to Bionaz in the Valpelline.   In mountaineering, traditionally used by climbers, leaving the Fenêtre de Durand for "tourists". See Rtes. 161, 163.

AROLETTA CHAIN

LK 1366.   A jagged granite ridge over 2 km. long enclosing the W side of the Crête Sèche cwm below the Col de Crête Sèche, and dividing the latter cwm from the Faudery cwm further W, itself the depression separating the more massive Morion chain.   An outstanding rock climbing area, approached from the Spataro biv. hut in 15-45 min. according to rte. Several names for principal ridge features are not shown on LK, and the names shown are either incorrect or not attached to the pts. indicated.   All the heights are suspect.   There are at least 25 first rate rock climbs and as many good scrambles on the E side of the chain, ranging from 100m. to 400m. in grades III, IV & V.   The W (Faudery) side, which is remote, has only a few rtes. to date and the potential for new rtes. of high quality is considerable here.   The state of exploration to 1970 is described excellently with sketch map, diagrams and photos in Alpi Pennine, vol. I, pp. 366-403.

COL D'AYACE   3040m.

COL DE FAUDERY   3032m.

LK 1366.   The first is a frontier pass about one km. SW of the Col de Crête Sèche, the second immediately S across a hollow containing the snowfield of the Aroletta gl.   The latter forms the neck dividing the upper N ends of the Aroletta and Morion chains. By these two passes a very direct rte. can be made from the Chanrion hut to the Valpelline (Oyace). F+. In fact, longer than the Col de Crête Sèche.

MONT DE LA BALME   3347m.

LK 1366. Hardly a summit, merely an upstanding shoulder on the frontier ridge before Mt. Gelé, but an important ridge junction marking the place where the Morion chain is detached S from the frontier ridge. Crossed or skirted by rtes. up Mt. Gelé (q. v.). First ascensionists of Mt. Gelé.

MONT GELÉ   3518.2m.

LK 1346, 1366. A dominant mtn. in this region, much courted despite the lack of quality rtes. Rock generally mediocre but the snow sections are pleasant though sometimes steep in places and icy, and can become badly crevassed in late season. Climbed quite often in spring by ski-mountaineers. First ascent: F. W. Jacomb with J. B. & M. Croz, 11 August, 1861. Second: E. Hoffmann-Burkhardt with S. Bessard, J. Fellay, 14 July, 1866.

<u>North-East Side and South-East Ridge</u>. The usual rte. from the Chanrion hut, mixed climbing, varied and interesting, stonefall in couloir after midday. PD. First ascent: E. F. M. Benecke, H. A. Cohen, 16 July, 1894.

163 From the Chanrion hut take the lower approach of Rte. 7, by the original track or the jeep road, and get on to the Otemma gl. above or below the rock wall at pt. 2357m. Depending on conditions here, sometimes awkward stone covered ice hollows and riblets to cross before the gl. debris can be reached properly, and normally better by the upper traverse along top of the rock wall (45 min. -1 h.). Cross the moraine and stone strewn gl. snout SSW, loose and unpleasant, to similar ground cut by outfalls from the Crête Sèche gl. Go up the R (W) side of the outfall streams and get on to the R lateral moraine (pt. 2523m. LK50) where a track coming from the Chermotane pastures is joined. Follow this moraine which peters out in the middle of the Crête Sèche gl. (Across the gl. SE is the opening to the Col de Crête Sèche). Straight ahead (SW) reach the foot of a large couloir, 500m. high, dropping from the Col de la Balme in the frontier ridge just R (W) of Mt. de la Balme, pt. 3347m. (1½ h.). Climb the couloir on snow with broken rock near the top, or use rocks on R side as far as possible (1½ h.). On the other side descend a little to the Mt. Gelé gl., then work along the rock base of the SE ridge to below the summit. Take a short crevassed snow slope, and finally on the R the terminal rock crest of the SE ridge (45 min., 4½ h. from Chanrion hut).

164 To avoid the couloir in descent, from the Col de la Balme descend snow slopes S towards the Col du Mt. Gelé for half the distance towards this col, to c. 3200m., then bear L over the broad ridge and descend a snow slope SE into the hollow of the Aroletta gl. (From here the adjoining Col d'Ayace could be taken, but the Swiss side is a steep, loose rock slope). At the bottom keep R and go down a gully carrying the outfall stream, normally snow, to exit L (N) over moraine and snow where Rte. 161 is joined near pt. 2751m. Follow this rte. to the Col de Crête Sèche and go down the Swiss side by debris to the Crête Sèche gl. which is descended easily to moraine below the Col de la Balme couloir, as on the approach rte. (descent thus to Chanrion hut, 3½ h.).

From Spataro Biv. Hut. A pleasant enough snow climb, F/F+. Starting by Rte. 161, join Rte. 164 to go up the couloir emerging at the Aroletta gl., then as for Rte. 164 (3 h. from biv. hut to summit). First ascensionists.

South Flank. The usual rte. from the By cwm, a bit tedious.

F/F+.

165 From the Regondi biv. hut cross the large scree terrace running NNE, passing round NW side of the Beuseya lake, then climb the debris terrace due E to reach moraines leading up towards pt. 2859m. at the base of the Morion peaks. After a fairly steep loose section continue by a rising traverse up the Mt. Gelé gl. to the N, rubble and snow, to slightly crevassed narrows at c. 3100m. (This pt. can also be reached by continuing along the large scree terrace, past pt. 2561m., into a broad scree couloir rising NE, in which the main outfall stream descends from the Gelé gl. Go right up to the top of it). Ascend snow slopes trending R, fairly steeply for a short distance then easing off just before the Col de la Balme where Rte. 163 is joined (3¼ h. from Regondi biv. to summit). From the slightly crevassed narrows, a direct line can be taken NNW to the summit if the snow is good, saving 15 min. or more.

166 North-West Face. About 650m. high, this broad rockface is cut fairly centrally and just R of the summit fall line by a prominent ice and rock couloir. The lower section on ice could be quite hard while the upper part has poor rock. Considerable stonefall danger - climbed solo by E. L. Fankhauser, 31 July, 1899. Probably unrepeated, grade D. L of the couloir the highest part of the rockface was climbed to exit directly at the summit by H. Bruchez, L. Troillet, 24 August, 1968. Similar climbing with very bad rock and pitches of IV and V (5 h. from foot of face). AJ 1974, p. 176. This rte. was repeated in winter by M. Bruchey, V. May, 3 January, 1975.

FENÊTRE DE DURAND   2797m.

LK 1346, 1366. The only true pedestrian pass across the frontier ridge in the Western Pennines before the Great St. Bernard road. Crossed since the middle ages with written accounts dating from the 16th century, from Mauvoisin (Chanrion hut) to the By cwm, Glacier roadhead, Ollomont and the Valpelline. Both sides with a footpath, F.

167 From the Glacier roadhead (1549m.), about 3 km. above Ollomont village (bus service), start outside the hamlet at the service cableway sta. On its L side a good path slants R (N) under the cableway just above the sta., and mounts steadily to cross the main river R (1670m.), then resumes a zigzag ascent N to a T junction near the Casa Farinet (2009m.) cableway terminus, just below the lower end of the By plain. Keep R, away from the small lake, along a small shoulder called the Cheval Blanc and take the next fork R (L for the By chalets), ascending gradually E to the Balme chalets (2128m.) (1¼ h.). Ignore turnings L and go under a rockband across a stream to continue by a good path E and ENE along to the Lombardi chalets (2321m.), then along the R side of a stream to a fork just before the Thoules chalets (2378m.). Keep L, traversing above these chalets, and so reach the main Acqua Bianca stream near pt. 2410m. (1 h.). Follow the stream on the L then the R side, due N, to where its tributaries from above converge. Cross R over stones where the path is vague. Above pt. 2470m. it becomes clear again and zigzags up grass and stony slopes to the icy Lago Fenêtre (2708m.). Passing along the N side of this small lake, the path over debris soon reaches the col (1¼ h., 3½ h. from Glacier roadhead; 2¾ h. in descent).

168 From the Chanrion hut descend the footpath due S for 10 min., past the junction for the Otemma gl. lower approach, to where it joins a section of sharp bends in the jeep road coming from below. By shortcuts mostly avoiding the road, go down into the main valley (La Barme), then downstream, crossing the road for the last time, to reach the footbridge at pt. 2185m. (30 min.). On the other side take the path on one big zigzag (2207m.) to the Grand Chermotane chalet (2255m.). Just after

174

this the trail divides. Go R up grass slopes in several zigzags generally SW, finally near a little stream at the top of the Plan Petit Giètro (c. 2520m.) which points the way clearly upwards at a moderate gradient into the trench (pt. 2657m.) between the mtn. side and an old lateral moraine bordering the Fenêtre gl. The path goes up this trench without possible error to stony ground, snow patches between rockbands and finally passes R (N) of a small mound marking the col (2 h., $2\frac{1}{2}$ h. from Chanrion hut; $2\frac{1}{4}$ h. in reverse direction).

Morion Chain

Catena del Morion. Quite the most impressive of the neglected sub ranges of the Western Pennines, in the course of early exploration trampled by numerous eager parties, not least the British. It remains rarely visited, shielded by long, steep and tiresome approaches, and after this welcomes the climber with a girdle of rotten rock and stonefall.

Only the Regondi biv. hut offers a base at reasonable altitude, on the W side of the chain, but from here it is too dangerous to attempt the principal summits. Much of the ridge detail is omitted by LK. This ridge is three times longer than the Aigs. Rouges d'Arolla and more than twice the length of the Bouquetins. Its complete traverse is longer than the integral Peuterey ridge of Mt. Blanc.

The rockface on the W (By cwm) side reaches a maximum height of 700m. and is continuously steep (60° average). On the E side the wall is up to 1100m. high, but is less steep and interesting and more broken. The crest carries countless peaklets and gendarmes, so thin in places that it is pierced by holes.

Climbing exploration did not start in earnest until the 1890s, and even by 1937 a 1600m. long section of the main ridge had not been traversed. The complete traverse of the Morion chain was first achieved by A. Miotti with T. Gobbi, 2-3 September, 1943. The summits of this chain are described below from N to S.

BECCA DI FAUDERY   3301m.

169 LK 1366. Bec de Faudery. Triangular rock peak easily climbed by its N ridge on unstable rock in 40 min. from the Col du Mt. Gelé. First ascent: Abbé Bionaz, J. Henry, 12 September, 1913.

BECCA CREVAYE   3320m.

170 LK 1366. Bec Crevaye. Separated from the Bca. di Faudery by a prominent ridge gap, Colle Bonacossa (c. 3220m., not marked on map), and from the more imposing Trident de

Faudery by the Colle della Becca Crevaye (3230m. IGM, not marked on map). Above the latter, the S ridge is marked by two secondary towers called P. Martinotti (c. 3280m.) and P. Gaia (c. 3282m.). The main N-S ridge has fairly good rock but the steep flanks are rotten, making access hazardous. Grade II/III pitches. First ascent: P. Bovet, J. Henry with T. Forclaz, 11 July, 1904.

TRIDENT DE FAUDERY   3384m.

LK 1366. Striking triple rock prongs dominating the N end of the Morion chain. "Jamais Trident ne mérita mieux son nom; c'est un des plus caractéristiques de toutes les Alpes" (Kurz). From N to S: Pta. Henry (3384m.), Pta. Ferrario (c. 3370m., not marked on map), Pta. Topham (3384m.). The dividing gaps are called simply Colle Ferrario and Colle Topham. Pta. Topham falls on the S side to Colle Bietti (3292m.). First ascents: Pta. Henry: P. Bovet, J. Henry, N. Tofani, 20 June, 1907. Pta. Ferrario: P. Ferrario, O. Schiavio, 30 July, 1914. Pta. Topham: A. G. Topham with J. Maître, P. Maurys, 26 July, 1893.

171 Pta. Henry   3384m.

W Flank. PD+, pitches of II. Serious. Stonefall in access couloir, possibly at other places as well. A high class "ordinary" outing, not in fact climbed often. From the Regondi biv. hut reach the foot of the Trident by Rte. 165 in 1½ h. A big snow couloir runs up to Colle Bietti (3292m.) on the R of Pta. Topham. Cross a bergschrund and climb the couloir for 120m., to where on the L side a gully/ledge system branches off steeply L, having already passed a similar weakness at 80m. up the couloir; the latter provides at a lower level a great diagonal line across all three Trident peaks to the col on N side of Pta. Henry, while the upper one now reached seems to cross most of the rock flank as well. These two great ramps are the most conspicuous features on this side of the mtn.

Follow this ramp L at a fairly high angle with snow patches to cross the delicate icy gully falling from Colle Topham (between Pta. Topham and Ferrario), and continue along the ramp line even more steeply across the rock wall of Pta. Ferrario, to reach the narrow couloir/chimney below Colle Ferrario. Ascend this keeping slightly R near the top, with several steep pitches, to the ridge gap. Now go up the loose, broken but easy rock of the broad S ridge to the top of Pta. Henry ($2\frac{1}{2}$ h. , 4 h. from Regondi biv.).

Note. The traverse of Pta. Henry, starting up the lower ramp line out of the Bietta couloir (see above) is about AD-, with pitches of II+. From the col on the N side you climb the N ridge keeping mainly on the R (W) side, on steep, rotten and often icy rock.

172 Pta. Ferrario   c. 3370m.

By the N ridge from Colle Ferrario (Rte. 171), short, III, good rock, summit block tricky, peg, IV. The near vertical S ridge on the other side, down to Colle Topham is descended by abseiling. Probably never climbed direct.

173 Pta. Topham   3384m.

While the first ascensionists' rte. is the only practical one, it is rendered quite hazardous by the obligatory ascent of the Bietti couloir. This is nearly 300m. high, reaches 50° in its steeper upper half, and is battered by frequent stonefall which only relents in very cold conditions. Technically, AD-. As for Rte. 171, and go right up couloir to top. Snow/ice not serious, but rock sections at the R side when taken to escape the path of stones are loose and delicate (2 h.). From Colle Bietti climb the blunt S ridge on very steep rock with plenty of holds, pleasant (II), making several movements on the E side (45 min. , $4\frac{1}{4}$ h. from Regondi biv. hut).

MORION NORTH   c. 3502m.

174 LK 1366.   The actual summit is hardly distinguishable in
relation to the complexity of peaklets formed along the main
part of the Morion ridge.   Bizarre history of confusion over
names and which summits were reached by the pioneers.
   After Colle Bietti (3292m.) the ridge gathers immediately
into a fine twin pronged gendarme called the Two Saints - Pta.
Judith and Pta. Esther (c. 3340m.), followed by several small
towers called the Sega del Morion.   Then a short regular
stretch of ridge mounts to the Morion North triplication.   Here,
the first top, called Pta. Baratono (3484m.), is the pt. marked
on map.   In close succession, the second is Pta. Augusto
(c. 3500m.), the third and highest, Pta. Monro (c. 3502m.),
this being the second highest pt. (just) in the Morion chain.
   Pta. Monro was first reached by W. D. Monro with A. Bovier
father & son, 11 September, 1895.   While the 2nd ascent was
made by an Italian only in 1924, he had to make the 3rd ascent
7 days later in order to continue N along the ridge to tread the
virgin tops of Pta. Augusto and Pta. Baratono: E. Enrico
with L. Carrel, C. Maquignaz, 7 July, 1924.   This short traverse has pitches of II & III on good rock.
   The only satisfactory way to reach Pta. Monro is to traverse
the main ridge from Morion Central.   This involves some very
bad rock, relieved by good patches, but with the crux at a
crumbling step (III+).   The last part is narrow and exposed
with pitches of III (1½ h. from Morion Central).   A fixed rope
should be placed for returning.   Rarely climbed.

MORION CENTRAL   3487m.

LK 1366.   The easiest but least distinctive of the three Morion
summit areas, it does offer a fairly straightforward rte. for
reaching the main ridge, but only on the monotonous E side.
First ascent: F. Baker-Gabb with C. Zurbriggen father &
son, 18 August, 1891.

<u>South-South-East Flank.</u>   A fairly long, continuously steep
ascent of little difficulty, monotonous, with stonefall in places.
Vertical interval from road, 2000m.   PD, on account of dur-
ation and rte. finding problems.   Pitches of II.   Descended by
A. G. Topham with J. Maître, P. Maurys,   18 July, 1895.
Ascended by F. Aston-Binns, P. Bovet, G. E. Wherry with
G. Bich, C. Zurbriggen son, 16 August, 1898.

175 In the Valpelline start from the road at 1500m. near chalets called Places (1490m.), a short distance below Chentre. Two faint tracks, one above the other, cross scrub pasture W and approach the Varrère torrent. Where the tracks meet a better track climbs in short zigzags N through open woodland to a small high pasture. After a ruined hut it fades out to the NE (R). Bear L and go up a stony grass slope N with a poor track, narrowing up to the foot of the SE ridge of Morion Central at pt. 2389m. (2¼ h.).

To the immediate L (W) is a stream bed ravine. Traverse L, rising a little across the top of this and below its continuation gully, going over steep grassy rocks by a sheep track which leads round into the huge and desolate headslope area under Morion Central and S. Ascend this tedious slope NW, avoiding several rockbands, trending L over grass and rocks, then taking a big stone slope (snow) direct, the R hand of a pair, to finish just R of rock toe pt. 2693m., at the foot of the SSE flank proper, and at the entrance to an obvious gully, discontinuous higher up (1¼ h.).

Move up the gully L (stonefall) and turn a steep pitch L. Then climb trending R and fairly directly up a series of broken zigzag ledges and rock steps to reach the SE ridge above a steep section. Follow the ridge until it gathers steeply again. Traverse L into a gully and follow this to a broken rock facet which is taken to the summit (3 h., 6½ h. from Valpelline road).

MORION SOUTH   c. 3505m.

LK 1366. Marked on LK as 3497m., in fact the IGM height. Morion Central (see above) is generally accepted as 3487m., and the South summit is at least 16m. higher. This then is the highest and most distinctive pt. in the chain. There is no direct rte. worth considering from the W (Regondi biv.) side. The first ever attempt on any summit in the Morion chain was made by O.G. Jones and C.G. Monro with guides in 1891, who got some distance up a gully to the L of pt. 2836m. before retreating from dreadful rock; this gully was climbed in 1930 and has probably been repeated only 3 or 4 times. The easiest and safest rte. remains by a traverse from Morion Central. First ascent: F. Aston-Binns, P. Bovet, G. E. Wherry with G. Bich, C. Zurbriggen son, 16 August, 1898, from Morion Central.

176 <u>By Ridge from Morion Central.</u> Reach Morion Central by Rte. 175. Either (best), follow the crest on fairly good rock, over a gap then several little towers (III) to a more prominent tower called Pta. Gallo (III), and from there by a short descent and reascent in two short steps to Morion South. Or, from the first gap follow a discontinuous ledge line over bad rock under the ridge towers to join the last two steps, II (1-1¼ h.).

MONT CLAPIER 3437m.

177 LK 1366. The fairly horizontal crest of this mtn. carries five peaklets of near equal height. The culminating pt. is at the NE end. The pt. 3437m. indicated on LK is 350m. distance SW of the highest and represents the lowest of the five. It is unknown whether the height has been ascribed to the wrong end of the summit ridge, or whether the height and position indicated is correct; if the latter, the NE top is some 25-30m. higher. First ascent: A. G. Topham with J. Maître, P. Maurys, 21 July, 1896.

The easiest rtes. up this mtn. are PD+, all of them unsatisfactory, loose and exposed to stonefall. The WNW ridge is much the best rte., a fine rock climb with good and bad rock. AD+ with pitches of III & IV, several variations possible. Partly climbed in 1923, direct by C. Ramella, A. Sgorbini, 31 May, 1942. Only 4 ascents to 1970, all parties roping down the same way. 1 h. from Regondi biv., 5 h. for ridge.

PUNTA FIORIO 3332m.

178 LK 1366. After Mt. Clapier the Morion chain descends regularly in a series of small tower/steps to Colle Fiorio (c. 3170m., not marked on map), before rising again to this pointed summit, the last of note in the chain.

Complicated approaches over steep stony ground, long and tedious, to finish up the SW flank. A lot of loose rock, but steep and sound at the top. The summit edifice on the SW/S side can only be attained by climbing a pitch of III and a terminal pitch of IV. First ascent: E. Canzio, F. Mondini, N. Vigna with G. Noro, 21 August, 1895.

The best rte. is the NNE ridge (III) from Colle Fiorio, but this can only be reached by a hard 5-6 h. walk from Oyace in the Valpelline, finishing up a gully L of pt. 2830m., exposed to stonefall (T. Ashby, T.G. Longstaff with P. Georges, J. Maître, P. Maurys, 25 August, 1897).

COMBIN AREA

Mountain bases

Panossière Hut   2660m.

LK 1326, 1346. Cabane de Panossière. SAC. Original hut
site is 100m. distant and slightly higher at 2671m. Situated
on the E bank lateral moraine of the Corbassière gl. and at
the foot of the Gd. Tavé. Present building new in 1970, warden
and simple restaurant service, 100 places.

179 From Fionnay cross the river bridge beside the main road
near the village centre (signpost) and take a path over fields
SW to a series of zigzags rising to moderate slopes at pt. 1818m.
Keep L and follow a fairly level section W to a few short zigzags on the R side of a rockband, high above big bends in the
main road below. At a shoulder on top of rockband take a L
fork (S), away from some chalets at 1959m., and continue up
a narrow plateau SE with several chalets, finally crossing to
the lower side of a parallel water supply channel at the Pierres
Rodzes, where the path traverses horizontally to the grassy
moraine valley entrance of Plan Goli at pt. 2233m. Keep L
here over a few rocks and cross a double stream to reach
pt. 2377m. The track divides. Either way, to R (W) or L (S)
leads to the Corbassière moraine at pt. 2638m. The R-hand
path is less steep, more usual and perhaps slightly longer.
Follow the big moraine path directly to the hut (4 h. from
Fionnay).

Brunet Hut   2103m.

LK 1326, 1346. Cabane Brunet. Property of the Geneva Mountain Federation. Door locked, 32 places, equipped for self
catering. Warden and key holder at Champsec village. Situated on a pleasant grassy promontory below the Sery pastures

and above the forest limits, $2\frac{1}{2}$ km. SSE of Lourtier village.

180 Accessible from Lourtier in the Val de Bagnes by a road suitable for small vehicles, all the way to hut. Taxi hire available. At the top of the large forest clearing (1617m.) above the Pléna Dzeu chalets, the continuation road is not yet shown on map. From here it follows the obvious jeep track symbol running in a straight line SE to a series of zigzags mounting to the hut promontory. On foot, about $3\frac{1}{2}$ h. A shorter but much steeper forest path can be taken from the main road some 2 km. above Lourtier, from bridge pt. 1335m., through the Clève forest and past Plan Tornay (1763m.) ($2\frac{1}{2}$ h.).

Valsorey Hut   3030m.

LK 1345, 1346, 1366. Cabane de Valsorey. SAC. Situated on the SW side of the principal Gd. Combin massif, in a fine position looking across to the Velan massif. The hut stands at the top of a long rock rib, immediately below moraine of the tiny Meitin gl. Warden sometimes resident, when a simple restaurant service might be provided. Door otherwise unlocked, fully equipped, 40 places.

181 From Bourg St. Pierre leave the village by a small road on L at the top (S) end, which undercrosses the main St. Bernard road and enters the Valsorey valley. Follow road to the Cordonna chalets (1834m.) (30 min.). Cars can be driven to this pt. and parked with discretion. Continue by a mule path with a very gradual ascent. Soon after crossing a prominent stream, reach a fork (signpost), just below pt. 2152m. Now go L and up to the Amont chalets (2197m.) ($1\frac{1}{2}$ h.). From here take the lower of two paths which mounts the Six Rodzes rockband (2352.5m.) before reaching open slopes called the Grands Plans (2501.8m.), below the Meitin cwm. Ascend NE over grass, stones and snow patches, path becoming poor, to a low relief rock spur, pt. 2614m. Work L on to this and follow its L side before moving R on to the easy crest, which leads to moraine where the hut is found. It is much further up the spur than appearances suggest from below ($2\frac{1}{2}$ h., $4\frac{1}{2}$ h. from Bourg St. Pierre).

Velan Hut 2569m.

LK 1345, 1346, 1366. Cabane du Velan. SAC. Situated near the W bank moraine of the Tseudet gl., directly N of Mt. Velan, and opposite the Valsorey hut, across the valley. Warden sometimes resident, when a simple restaurant service might be provided. Door otherwise unlocked, fully equipped, 55 places.

182 From Bourg St. Pierre proceed as for Rte. 181 and reach the second of two junctions in the path, not far below the Amont chalets. Take the R fork (signpost), cross the river (2152m.) and follow a good path to cross a tributary stream (2257m.), above which the path gathers into a series of zigzags at a comfortable gradient on a stony slope, finishing on the W lateral moraine of the Tseudet gl. Follow the moraine for a short way to reach hut on the R ($3\frac{1}{2}$ h. from Bourg St. Pierre).

Bourg St. Bernard 1914m.

183 LK 1365. At the N tunnel entrance on the Gt. St. Bernard road. Piste skiing area for winter sports, called Super St. Bernard, dominated by the Menouve cableway. Small hotels open in summer.

ITALIAN

Amiante Hut 2979m.

LK 1366. Rifugio Amiante. CAI. A small and old hut situated on a rocky plateau at the top of the By cwm and below the Gde. Tête de By. Fully equipped but advisable to take your own stove, 12 places. Door normally locked, keys with warden at Ollomont village.

184 From Glacier roadhead (1549m.) above Ollomont follow

Rte. 167 to the fork at the inner end of the Cheval Blanc. Take the L branch (N) across the By plain to the By chalets (2048m.) ($1\frac{1}{4}$ h.). Turn R after the first or second building to join a track winding NE over pasture to a vague fork. Keep L and traverse in the same direction to cross a stream, then go up gradually L, path vague, to some old barracks (2302m.). From here the track progressively worsens, making a long slanting movement NW under Pta. Ratti, over two streams, to reach a shoulder under a little cliff where it turns N along the L (W) side of a grassy rock spur (2700m.). Follow the R side of an old stream bed under the spur, twisting up steeply with few signs of a track, to a stony slope below a line of cliffs. Go up to the L end of these cliffs and bear round R to a debris plain above. Move R (E) to reach the hut almost horizontally in a few min. ($2\frac{3}{4}$ h. , 4 h. from Glacier roadhead).

Variation. A more direct and recommended way up the last section alongside the spur is to leave the original track line before spur, at c. 2660m. , where it traverses L to go round a little bluff before turning N. Instead, climb straight up grass and rock slopes on the R (E) side of spur, near a stream bed further R. Follow line of latter up to the L end of a big cliff facing S, whose R end is marked by a waterfall, above which lies the debris plain and hut. Climb the L end of the cliff by easy slabs, so reaching the head of the spur and lower SW end of the debris plain simultaneously. Move R to reach hut in 200m. distance.

Savoie Bivouac 2668m. 2651m. IGM

LK 1366. Bivacco Savoie. Marked but not named on map. Property of the Aosta region tourist board, supervised by the CAI, erected in 1965. A tiny wooden shelter with basic equipment, door open. Take your own stove. Situated on the grassy spur above Colle Boegno Bà, rising into the SE ridge of Les Trois Frères, thus the ridge enclosing the W side of the By cwm.

185 From Glacier roadhead (1549m.) above Ollomont follow Rte. 167 to the T junction under the Cheval Blanc. Take the L fork up to Casa Farinet, and cross the barrage wall of the small lake to the W side. A good path rises gradually W through open trees to a T junction. Go L to just above the Porchère chalets (2094m.), with another junction. Turn back R up grassy slopes where paths are several and worn by roaming cattle, and reach a water supply channel. From here ascend L (NW), mounting steadily under little rockbands below the broad spur of the Dosso Boegno Bà. The path remains good and eventually approaches the valley bed and stream on the L. Follow a rather discontinuous track up the grassy R side of the stream, passing just above the level of an obvious little plain on the other side (2533m.), where there is a better track. Now slant R on to a broad grassy rib and follow this to where it shortly merges into the final grassy part of the spur above the Colle Boegna Bà. Traverse R for 100m. to the biv. hut (3 h. from Glacier roadhead).

Grand Combin Group

North of the Col de Sonadon, the most impressive ice massif in the Western Pennines and the only part of the western range to exceed 4000m. It affords mostly general mountaineering interest in the lower and middle grades.

GRAND TAVÉ 3158.2m.

LK 1346. Peaklet standing above the Panossière hut, often climbed as an afternoon walk. Splendid view. First known tourist ascent: W. G. Hutchinson with two unnamed guides, 31 August, 1886.

186 <u>Normal Routes</u>. F/F+. From Panossière hut descend a little N and follow track round N end of a rockband, to where it commences steep zigzags towards the Col des Otanes. At top of zigzags leave the track and bear R up the E scree and rock slopes of the mtn., variable ways, and reach the summit direct ($1\frac{1}{2}$ h.). Or from the Col des Otanes (2846m.), cross scree and snow to some rocks which are skirted under pt. 3078m., followed by a short scramble L to the broad N ridge leading briefly to summit (2 h.). Or at the bottom go round S end of rockband and climb a scree slope headed by a gully, to reach the S ridge, which gives a steep but easy rock climb to the top ($1\frac{1}{4}$ h.). For a simple traverse, go along S ridge to the Tavé des Chasseurs (3165m.) and the Col de Bocheresse (3102m.), easy, then descend rock and scree gully W to the Corbassière gl. moraine. E. F. M. Benecke, H. A. Cohen, 20 July, 1894.

TOURNELON BLANC 3707m.

LK 1346. Magnificent viewpoint and a popular training climb in the vicinity of the Panossière hut. First ascent: probably J. Gillioz, in 1865. F. Hoffmann-Merian with S. Bessard, J. Fellay, 5 July, 1867.

<u>North Ridge</u>. The usual rte., varied mixed climbing. PD-.

187 From the Panossière hut follow a track S along the Corbassière gl. moraine to debris slopes under the gully rising due E to the Col de Bocheresse. Climb into the next gully immediately R of this one, and go up it for 200m. to a line of weakness on the R, along the base of the W face of the Becca de la Lia. Above the base two steep ramps cross this face diagonally R. Follow the upper one, running parallel below the ridge above, over successively interesting rocks - gneiss, quartzite, schists, all easy, to finish on the S ridge of the Becca de la Lia. Descend a little and move L on to the snow saddle pt. 3365m. (2 h.). Alternatively, the lower diagonal ramp, narrower, can be climbed to a little snow tongue directly adjoining saddle 3365m. Now climb the broad pleasant snow ridge to a thin terminal crest and the summit (1 h., 3 h. from Panossière hut).

<u>South-West Ridge</u>. Normally used in descent, for traversing the mtn. Sometimes badly crevassed. F/F+.

188 From the Panossière hut follow a track S along the Corbassière gl. moraine to snow under the W side of the mtn. Continue up crevassed gl. slopes SW and round rock pt. 3140m., sérac debris from above. Now climb the broken snow slopes, sometimes with long crevasses but otherwise easy, to the snow saddle above (E), Col du Tournelon Blanc (3538m.) (2¾ h.). Go up shingle and scree/snow to N, and turn snow dome 3630m. on R to reach a broad saddle 3595m. Continue along the broad snow/shale ridge to broken rock under S side of summit. Mount directly to top (45 min., 3½ h. from Panossière hut; 2 h. in descent).

GRAND COMBIN   4314m.

LK 1346, 1366.   An immense mtn. block having an aloofness akin to the Himalaya. It yields in height to no mtn. group in the Alps save Mt. Blanc and Mte. Rosa. For a long time one of the least known of major Alpine summits, the Gd. Combin is a massif in itself with several distinct summits over 4000m. which crown the head of the Corbassière gl., the longest ice stream in the Western Pennines. The eponymous satellites of the massif are a group of peaks isolated further N, above the W bank of the gl. The climbing is mainly on snow and ice but there are several interesting rock scrambles, though much of the rock is loose shale.

The picturesque N side is distinguished by a system of huge gl. terraces, separated by snow plateaux which provide the normal approaches from the Panossière hut. A considerable distance is covered from hut to the foot of the mtn. while all the terrain is snow or ice with hardly a rock to touch for 6 to 8 h. The shortest rtes. come up from Bourg St. Pierre via the Valsorey hut, and have an equal amount of snow and rock work. The Ital. approaches are rarely followed but the recommended rte. is a fine expedition.

The first 4 parties to climb the mtn. attained the Aig. du Croissant (4243m.), mistaking it for the highest pt., an error due largely to the adamant opinion of local guides. It is unexplained why at least one of these parties in perfect weather could not ascertain or continue to reach a clearly higher summit only 30 min. away. These ascents were made in 1857-58, the second (1857) by W. Mathews, who had already been taken up the Corbassière the previous year because it was thought to be the highest pt. of the Gd. Combin massif. The highest pt., the Grafeneire, was finally trodden by C. St. C. Deville with D., E. & G. Balleys, B. Dorsaz, 30 July, 1859. Daniel Balleys was once criticised by a client for being too cautious, but this admonition was answered by E. W. Bowling: "Balley has the good fortune, or bad fortune (who can tell?) to own a wife and some 12 or 13 little Balleys, and for their sakes and for his own sake, as well as for the sake of his future employers, it is to be hoped that he will continue to show the caution which is essential in a good guide ..." First British (second) ascent: W. E. Utterson-Kelso with Deville's guides, 4 August, 1859. In winter, partly on ski: M. Kurz, F. F. Roget with M. Crettez, 31 March, 1907.

First ascents of the other main summits. De Valsorey: J. H. Isler with J. Gillioz, 16 September, 1872. By a British party: E. W. Bowling, H. White with D. Balleys, M. Balmat, H. Dévouassoud, 2 September, 1874. De la Tsessette: E. F. M. Benecke, H. A. Cohen, 21 July, 1894.

COMBIN DE TSESSETTE   4141m.

LK 1346.   The lowest of the three main tops of the massif, at its E end.   Seen from the N, it does not look much and represents a large gl. step at one edge of the terrace system at the head of the Corbassière gl.   Rarely climbed for itself and normally included with an ascent of the Grafeneire.

<u>West Ridge</u>.   A short, easy detour from the ordinary Grafeneire rte.   Effectively, PD-/PD.   Rewarding view.   First ascensionists.

189 From the Panossière hut, as for Rte. 192 to the Col du Croissant (4090m.).   Move L (E) over a snow hump (4121m.) and in the same direction along a broad snow walkway to the summit in 20 min.   Or shorter, below the col, traverse easily away from the usually big crevasse there and continue rising a little over snow to top (about $5\frac{1}{2}$ h. from hut).

190 <u>North-East Face</u>.   The highest and most extensive wall in the Combin massif, 1200m. above the Tsessette gl.   Characterised by delicate climbing over long stretches of bad rock with several difficult sections on ice near the top;   bad stonefall.   A line up the L side of the face, starting near pt. 2864m. was climbed by R. Fellay, M. Machoud, 19 August, 1943 in $7\frac{1}{2}$ h.   Unrepeated, probably D.   A more direct line starting just R of pt. 2893m. at a snow tongue, and called the Central Spur, was climbed by M. Bruchez, A. & V. May, 5-7 July, 1974, probably TD (LA 1975, Quarterly issue, pp. 115-6). Starting at R side of snow tongue dividing the Central Spur (L) and a R-hand spur, the latter spur was climbed by M. Bruchez, A. May exactly 2 years later, 5-7 July, 1976.   TD with pitches

of IV+ and V (LA 1977, Monthly bulletin, p. 17. Rte. diagram
and descriptions).

TOUR DE BOUSSINE   3883m.

191 LK 1346. Outlying to SE of the Combin de Tsessette, huge
shoulder pyramid of rock and ice, the object of "elimination"
rtes. in recent years, now ascended by all of its faces and
ridges. Little real interest, poor rock and the faces are raked
by stonefall. First ascent: J. J. Weilenmann with J. Gillioz,
20 July, 1867, by SSE ridge (PD).

COMBIN DE GRAFENEIRE   4314m.

LK 1346, 1366. The culminating pt. of the massif, one of the
quintessential snow climbs of the Alps, analagous in gl. features and nomenclature to the N side of Mt. Blanc, albeit on a
smaller scale.

<u>From North (Mur de la Côte)</u>. The ordinary rte. on this side,
and in former days also the normal way from the SW side
(Bourg St. Pierre) by crossing the Col des Maisons Blanches.
The latter is hardly ever used now. The rte. crosses the N
flank from R to L (SE) using a system of slanting gl. plateaux.
Normally a beaten trail in summer but all this ground is bad
for rte. finding in poor weather and white outs. The problems
are those of intricate gl. terrain which varies from year to
year. PD. First ascensionists.

192 From the Panossière hut follow the moraine S for 5 min. ,
then descend to the gl. and cross it SW to reach the W side at
2700m. Follow up this side keeping close to the flank of the
Combin de Corbassière. Crevasses increase in number as
height is gained but moraine strips assist progress up to beside
pt. 3155.5m. Ahead is a badly broken gl. band under the
Plateau des Maisons Blanches. Ascend SW towards pt. 3310m. ,
turning the most crumpled section on the R. So reach at its

N end the extensive gl. plateau under the impressive pinnacled chain of the Maisons Blanches (3 h.). Move across the plateau S towards the Col du Meitin, then work gradually L (E), passing about 350m. distance S of pt. 3406.2m., over an upper and final large snow terrace called the Plateau de Déjeuner. This narrows into the first sloping snowband rising SE above the huge crescent-shaped rockband lying at the N foot of the mtn. Keep near its L edge and go up the snowband, called the Corridor, also keeping near its outer edge. At a relatively narrow place halfway up you are exposed to falling ice from the R, where a crown of séracs extends along the top of the parallel Mur de la Côte. Emerge on a broad slope at a moderating gradient, trend L (E) to avoid a ruptured section (large crevasse), and return R (S) to arrive immediately below the Col du Croissant (4090m.). To the R (SW) is the apex snow/ice facet of the Mur de la Côte (2 h.).

Climb the Mur slope at 45° for 50m., slanting from L to R so as to pass below the shoulder at its head, on to gentle snow slopes under the Aig. du Croissant. Large cornice possible at this exit, usually avoidable by climbing steeply a short distance L before returning R. Now either circle back L and R (generally SE), turning the end of a large bergschrund above, and mount the moderately steep, rounded snow spur going up to the Aig. du Croissant (4243m.), and from its summit taking the main ridge S with large cornice on L (E) side, into a depression, then up a similar ridge to the summit. Or, more usual, cross the moderate snow slopes SW below the Aig. du Croissant bergschrund, descending a little in order to turn a huge continuation crevasse, then go up a small snow hollow still further SW to emerge under the topmost crest of the W ridge within a few m. of the summit; keep R to finish. One may also take an intermediate line into the ridge depression between the Aig. du Croissant and the summit ($1\frac{1}{2}$-2 h., $6\frac{1}{2}$-7 h. without halts from Panossière hut, about $4\frac{1}{2}$ h. in descent).

194

GRAND COMBIN N side

Tsessette
4141

Croissant Grafeneire
col 4243 4314
4121 4090

Valsorey
4184.4

Col du Tournelon
Blanc
3538

3630

188

192

193

192

189

M. de la Gliète

Corbatta

G.d Combin gl.

188

3163

188

Corbassière gl.

3766

4140

4282

<u>West Ridge (from Combin de Valsorey).</u> A simple connection
and link for rtes. initially reaching the Valsorey summit. F+.

193 From the Valsorey summit descend on the R by a short,
sharp and steep snow crest (cornice) then leave it conveniently
to keep L, down to saddle pt. 4132m. Continue up the snow
ridge keeping L so that just below the top you enter the little
snow hollow rising into the summit. Trend L to reach the top,
cornice (45 min.).

<u>South-East Ridge.</u> Although situated in Switzerland and ap-
proached from the vicinity of the Col du Sonadon, this ridge
offers the most direct rte. from Italy. Longer from the Valsorey hut. Mixed climbing of considerable interest, varied,
with outstanding scenery and situations, one of the best expeditions of its class in the Pennine Alps. Serious, but in good
conditions it will present no problems for a competent party.
PD+ in good conditions, friable rock. First ascent: O. G. Jones
with A. Bovier, P. Gaspoz, 10 September, 1891.

194 From the Amiante hut cross shale and debris due N to
snowbeds running up L (NW) to the base of the Gde. Tête de By.
Ascend in the middle, turning a low rockband on the L, then
work N again to the obvious ridge saddle of the <u>Col d'Amiante</u>
(3308m.) under the Gde. Tête (1 h.). On the other side descend
a snow hollow running into the Mt. Durand gl. and cross a gl.
terrace in the same N direction at c. 3250m., towards pt. 3152m.
which marks the W foot of the SE ridge. As soon as possible
bear L up a crevassed gl. bank above, ascending NW towards
the Col du Sonadon. Before reaching an outcrop in line with
the col, turn R up the snow slope between this outcrop and the
slanting base of the ridge now on your R. So mount this slope
on the S side of the ridge (1¼ h.).

Coming from the Valsorey hut, reach the Col du Sonadon by
Rte. 195, descend a little then traverse snow under the first

part of the SSW ridge branch of the SE ridge, rising well above the outcrop mentioned above, into the middle of the S side snow slope ($3\frac{1}{2}$ h.).

Climb straight up snow to c. 3600m., then trend R up a series of debris bands, and zigzag up these with alternate snowbeds keeping R, to the top of the uppermost large triangular snow patch. Ascend a final sweep of easy slabs to reach the ridge crest not far above a little rock step, pt. 3946m. Follow the crest to a gendarme/step and turn this L along a ledge line to rejoin the progressively narrowing ridge which becomes a sharp snow crest rising at a good angle to another rock step 100m. higher. Alternatively, follow an edge of rocks under L side of crest to same place. Traverse about 12m. L along base of step to a short, wide chimney and climb this (5m., II, loose) to a rather longer second chimney (III-), and exit on a ledge. Now move up delicately R along the edge of a slabby rib (II+), above which a blocks pitch of very steep loose rock leads back to the crest at the top of the step. Follow a fine snow crest in an airy position to below the summit cornice. Normally traverse delicately L for 25m. along the top of a rock wall, then climb back R up a steep snow pitch to emerge at the top of the W ridge a few steps from the summit (4 h., $6\frac{1}{4}$ h. from Amiante hut; $7\frac{1}{2}$ h. from Valsorey hut).

COL DU SONADON   3504m.

LK 1346, 1366. Between the Combin de Grafeneire and Le Sonadon, an important gl. pass for linking rtes. on the S side of the Gd. Combin, for access across the adjoining Swiss/Ital. frontier (By cwm), and not least as a key passage in the High Level Rte. from Chamonix to Zermatt, this section tradition-ally having the reputation of being the crux of that journey for skiers. See <u>High Level Route</u> (Roberts, 1973). First traverse: F. W. Jacomb with J. B. & M. Croz, 7 August, 1861.

195 From the Valsorey hut take a small track with cairns NE

MT. DURAND GL.

Mt. Avril
3346.9
210

2735.7

Col de By
3189

Tête Blanche
3418
211

Gd. Tête de By
3587.8
212

Col d'Amiante
3308
194

3094

196

Chanrion hut

over scree and snow to the Meitin gl. snowfield and to the foot
of a rock rib which borders the L (W) side of the couloir coming
down from the Col du Meitin. From here slant progressively
R (E) and climb fairly steep snow and broken rock to a snow
saddle which overlooks a large snowfield called the Plateau du
Couloir, under the S face of the Combin de Valsorey. The
saddle is normally attained some 150-200m. N of pt. 3664m.,
at a somewhat higher level and close to the foot of the SW rib
of the Combin de Valsorey ($2\frac{1}{4}$ h.). Now descend the snow
plateau ESE, stonefall possible, and go down a short steep
section constricted by the ends of two rockbands, crevassed,
bergschrund probable, on to the last snowfield of the Sonadon
gl. Cross this in the same direction to a short riser and the
col (45 min., 3 h. from Valsorey hut, 2 h. in descent). PD-.

196 From the Chanrion hut descend to the Barme bridge
(2185m.), go up to the Grand Chermotane chalet (2255m.) and
take the Fenêtre de Durand path as for Rte. 168, as far as the
little stream at the top of the Plan Petit Giètro (c. 2520m.).
Leave the path of Rte. 168, cross the stream and traverse
slopes N with a small discontinuous track for a few min. About
300m. distance away from the grassy ridge corner ahead, turn
L (SW) and ascend in a hollow to a small opening in the ridge
just R (N) of pt. 2735.7m. (Immediately below the SW turning
pt. a track can be seen going straight down rough grass slopes,
bypassing the Gd. Chermotane chalet, to the Barme bridge at
the bottom; recommended for descent). From the ridge opening a trench runs horizontally SW beside pt. 2697m. Just
beyond this pt. contour moraine banks with a slight descent
due W, in a few min. along the top of a rockband which peters
out into the lateral moraine slopes merging into the Mt. Durand
gl. at c. 2700m. Ascend the L side of the gl. SW over snow
slopes with a few crevasses and pass below a rock island under
the base (3094m.) of the Tête Blanche. Now almost in the

middle of the Mt. Durand gl., keep more to the L and ascend slopes in a hollow towards the Gde. Tête de By, going up the L side of a crevassed section with séracs on to a gl. terrace at c. 3250m. Cross this terrace horizontally N towards the foot (3152m.) of the Grafeneire SE ridge. Some 300m. distance before this pt. bear L up the N end of a crevassed bank above. So reach the last gl. hollow giving access to the col over easy snow NW ($5\frac{1}{2}$ h. from Chanrion hut, $3\frac{1}{2}$ h. in descent). F/F+.

COMBIN DE VALSOREY   4184.4m.

LK 1346. This westerly top of the Gd. Combin is easily the most interesting of the three main summits. Nearly all parties continue to the Grafeneire by the connecting ridge between the two, Rte. 193.

South-West Rib/Flank. The original "normal" rte. from the Bourg St. Pierre side of the mtn. It has fallen into disuse due to rising popularity for the harder but safer W ridge. Quite interesting and fairly steep all the way, mixed climbing with some stonefall danger after midday. PD. First ascensionists. Second ascent (British): F.T. Wethered with U. Almer and a porter, 27 August, 1878.

197 From the Valsorey hut follow Rte. 195 to the Plateau du Couloir ($2\frac{1}{4}$ h.). Above is a steep rock rib marking the angle between the SW facet and SSW face of the mtn. Start up the SSW side about 80m. R of the rib line, going up a broken slabby rockband then across a snowband to another stretch of rock still the same distance from the rib. At the top of this another broader snowband with ribs is followed to a rockband extension coming from the middle section of the W ridge. Ascend shallow snow gullies or their dividing ribs to the snow slope band extending below the upper snow shoulder of the W ridge. Up to this pt. nearly all the rock sections are loose and alternative

200

GRAND COMBIN SW side

Grafeneire

Valsorey

193

197

Plateau du Couloir

195

198

Meitin gl.

Valsorey hut

191

196

COL DU MEITIN

COMBIN DU MEITIN

snowy parts should be sought. Ascend diagonally R on snow
to the last rock step in the W ridge. Turn this on the R side
and go up steep broken rock to return L at the top of the step.
So reach the Valsorey summit in a few min. $(2\frac{1}{2}$-3 h. , $4\frac{3}{4}$-$5\frac{1}{4}$ h.
from Valsorey hut).

<u>West Ridge (from Col du Meitin)</u>. The most satisfactory rte.
from the Valsorey hut. The ridge rises in three unequal rock
steps, the first being highest and the other two progressively
shorter.   PD with short pitches of II+, rock mostly good and
the climbing interesting throughout. First ascent: C. Boisviel
with D. Balleys, S. Henry, 1 September, 1884.

198 From the Valsorey hut take a small track with cairns NE
over scree and snow to the Meitin gl. snowfield and to the foot
of a rock rib which borders the L (W) side of the couloir coming
down from the Col du Meitin.   Climb this rib by rocks and
scree, supplied with an intermittent track, and so reach the
col (3611m.) $(1\frac{3}{4}$ h.). In descent, it is quicker to use the scree
on the true L (opposite) side of the couloir.

From the Panossière hut follow Rte. 192 to the Plateau des
Maisons Blanches (3 h.), then steer due S across the snowfield to a bergschrund and short snow slope leading to the col
(45 min. , $3\frac{3}{4}$ h.).

From the col the first step is seen as a R-angled pillar.
Climb on the crest, turning the steepest parts on the R (S) side.
Continue thus to just below the tip of the roof-like pillar, then
slant L below an overhang. Having turned it, return to the
crest as soon as possible by a chimney. So reach a stony
(snow) shoulder and mount it to the foot of the second step.
Move R into a couloir marked by whitish rock and climb it to
the snow saddle below the third step. Cross this keeping a
little R of crest. Now either climb the third step direct (pitch
of III), or move to the R side and go up steep broken rock to
return L at the top of the step. So reach the Valsorey summit
202

in a few min. (3-4 h. , $4\frac{3}{4}$-$5\frac{3}{4}$ h. from Valsorey hut; $6\frac{3}{4}$-$7\frac{3}{4}$ h. from Panossière hut).

<u>North-West Face</u>. A narrow, slightly scooped face bordered R by a long rock rib (3628m.), affording the only modern pure ice climbing challenge on the mtn. An assortment of ice obstacles and a short rock headwall to finish. The angle varies between 40°-60°. Threatened by falling ice from séracs. 600m., D/D+. First ascent, L-hand exit: E. R. Blanchet with K. Mooser, 20 July, 1933. Second ascent, direct finish: E. Eidher, E. Vanis, 21 May, 1958. First British ascent: S. Bright, R. K. Roschnik, P. F. Rowat, 23 August, 1970 (6 h.). In winter with Blanchet exit: M. Dandelot, J. Jenny, 12 January, 1973. Climbed about 30 times to date.

199 From the Panossière hut reach the foot of the face by Rtes. 192, 198 in $3\frac{1}{4}$ h. From the Valsorey hut by Rte. 198 over the Col du Meitin in $2\frac{1}{4}$ h.

Start at the centre foot of the face and climb an ice slope cut by several schrunds. The slope gets progressively steeper and soon reaches a notable ice bulge giving a pitch of 60°. All this first section is exposed to possible discharges from ice cliffs to the R. Above the bulge trend L to an easier slope, cross another schrund and climb straight up to a rock outcrop with a good resting place on top. From here a thin snow/ice rib at 45° leads to a steeper short ice slope and the final rocks, where a good stance can be found. Somewhat L of the summit line, climb a narrow, shallow snow/ice couloir through the rocks, possibly with a pitch of 60°, to the top (5-7 h. for face).

The original Blanchet exit veers off L alongside the rock outcrop and exits L up an icy gully/depression in the side wall to reach the plateau area L of the summit headwall. Sometimes easier.

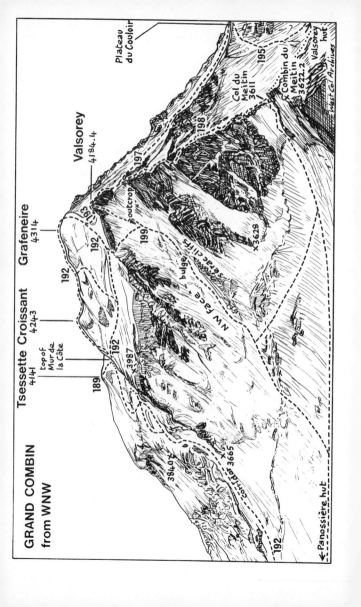

GRAND COMBIN
from WNW

Tsessette Croissant Grafeneire Valsorey
4141   4243   4314   4184.4

Plateau du Couloir

Col du Meitin 3611

Combin du Meitin 3622.2

Valsorey hut

West Col Archives

195¹

198

197

193

192

192

outcrop

199

X3628

top of Mur de la Côte

189

3987

3840

NW face

sérac cliffs

X 3665

Couloir du

192

← Panossière hut

COMBIN DU MEITIN   3622.2m.

LK 1346. A big step in the ridge between the Combin de Valsorey and the Maisons Blanches. No interest.

COL DES MAISONS BLANCHES   3418m.

200 LK 1346. Between the Combin du Meitin and the Maisons Blanches, an easy gl. pass between Bourg St. Pierre and the Panossière hut, from the former once the normal way of reaching the Gd. Combin - before the Valsorey hut was built. First crossing: D. & E. Balleys, A. & S. Dorsaz, 18 July, 1858.

LES MAISONS BLANCHES   3682m.

201 LK 1346. An impressive ridge of small rock peaks extending from the Col des Maisons Blanches to the Col de Boveire. The ridge has only been fully explored in the last 50 years. The difficulty and quality of the rock are very uneven, and the various peaks seem to be seldom visited. The highest pt. , Grande Aiguille, was first climbed by M. Maglioni with D. Balleys, N. Knubel, 23 June, 1874.

COL DE BOVEIRE   3495m.

LK 1346. Between the Maisons Blanches and the Combin de Boveire, a fine gl. pass from the Gt. St. Bernard road between Liddes and Bourg St. Pierre to the Panossière hut. Occasionally reached on the latter side for climbing the Combin de Boveire. First crossed in 1867.

COMBIN DE BOVEIRE   3663.1m.

LK 1346. The most southerly and least visited of the three Combin satellite summits. A gable top elevation with typically mixed terrain on the ridges and generally loose rock on the faces. First ascent: R. Broft with J. & O. Balleys, 1888.

202 By Various Ridges. All the ridges, W (from Col de

Boveire), N (from Col de Panossière), E (from pt. 3355m.)
are F+. The latter is the shortest way from the Panossière
hut. It is steeper than the other ridges and has more interest.
By Rte. 192 to foot of ridge (3355m.) in $2\frac{1}{2}$ h. First ascend
on R side then follow crest to a steep loose rock section leading
to the NE branch of the ridge, where the latter with a corniced
snow crest is taken to the top ($1\frac{1}{4}$ h., $3\frac{3}{4}$ h. from hut).

COL DE PANOSSIÈRE   3459m.

LK 1346. Between the Combin de Boveire and the Aigs. de
Boveire, a complementary and similar pass to the Col de Boveire (see above), rather more direct than latter. Rarely
crossed. First traversed by W. A. B. Coolidge, F. Gardiner
with C. & R. Almer, 10 August, 1890.

AIGUILLES DE BOVEIRE   3640m.

LK 1346. A series of rock peaks forming the true watershed
at a tangent to the spurs carrying the Combin de Corbassière
and Petit Combin. Rarely visited.

COMBIN DE CORBASSIÈRE   3715.5m.

LK 1346. An important mtn. in the Panossière hut region and
a fairly popular climb. It can be combined with the Petit Combin without much difficulty. First ascent: G. Studer with J. B.
Fellay, J. von Weissenfluh, 14 August, 1851. Second (British)
ascent, party misled into thinking they were going up the highest
pt. in the Gd. Combin massif: C. E. & W. Mathews with B. &
F. L. Fellay, A. Simond, 18 August, 1856.

South Ridge. The usual rte., a rather dull climb on mostly
sound rock. PD-. First ascent: C. Herzog, S. Junod, H.
Moulin, P. Wittnauer with J. Bessard, 20 July, 1889.

203 From the Panossière hut cross to the W side of the Corbassière gl. as for Rte. 192. Pass below the first opening

(2759m.) to a gl. tongue above, then below a gully in the rockband above. Now ascend diagonally L over scree to slant up the rockband in the same direction by little gullies and ledges, to reach a debris terrace on top. Above, ascend the gl. tongue in a big zigzag R then L, crevassed, to mount the general gl. slope SW, under the E face of the mtn., and at the top reach a snow saddle (3405m.) at the foot of the ridge ($2\frac{1}{4}$ h.). Follow the easy rock ridge to the snowhead summit ($1\frac{1}{4}$ h., $3\frac{1}{2}$ h. from hut).

<u>West Ridge.</u>   The usual way down, F+.   Descended by first ascensionists.

204 From the Panossière hut follow Rte. 192 to the crevassed slopes alongside pt. 3155.5m., then work NW into the large gl. bay under SW side of the mtn. Ascend into the top L (NW) corner where a shale and snow slope leads to saddle 3563m. From here follow the easy snow ridge to summit ($4\frac{1}{2}$ h. from hut, $2\frac{3}{4}$ h. in descent). The SW flank can be climbed almost anywhere by steep, loose but easy rock. Saddle 3564m. at the foot of upper part of W ridge can be reached quite easily from gl. bay below - shorter.

<u>North-West Face.</u>   A worthwhile snow climb, probably icy after mid season. AD. First ascent: M. Dandelot, J. Michel, P. von Siebenthal, 9 July, 1969.

205 From the Panossière hut cross the Corbassière gl. immediately to the W side and reach a snow/rock gully rising above pt. 2620m. Climb this to the S branch of the Follats gl., and go up its R side under a long rockband. The gl. is sometimes badly crevassed but the rock can be used without difficulty at various places. So reach an upper detached rockband ridge at pt. 3334m. Now cross the gl. S, rising to a bergschrund under the NW face, on the L of a sérac wall. (In some seasons, when the crevasses are less numerous, the L side of the gl., under the Combin de Corbassière, can be followed below the bergschrund line, all the way to the foot of the face). Ascend the snow face direct and somewhat L of the summit line to join the snowy NE ridge, cornice on other side, which is followed for 10 min. to the top ($4\frac{1}{2}$ h. from hut).

PETIT COMBIN   3672m.

LK 1346. The most interesting but on the whole least accessible of the Combin satellites. The N side rtes. are best approached from the Brunet hut. First recorded ascent: C. de la Harpe, E. W. Viollier with J. Bessard, 25 July, 1890. Second (British) ascent: W. A. B. Coolidge, F. Gardiner with C. & R. Almer, 10 August, 1890.

206 From the Panossière hut follow Rte. 204 to saddle 3563m., then cross the snow basin NNW above the Follats gl. to reach the summit snowcap on its L (W) side. Move up R to the top ($4\frac{1}{2}$ h. from hut).

<u>South Flank Direct</u>. A short cut for Rte. 206, up the Follats gl., generally used for ascent and descent until the crevasses become troublesome after mid season. PD.

207 From the Panossière hut follow Rte. 205 to pt. 3334m. The worst crevasses are now below. If necessary, the upper part of the rockband below this pt., which has a snowy crest, can be followed along edge of N branch of gl. From pt. 3334m. either continue up the mild gl. slopes into the basin at the top where Rte. 206 is joined just below the summit snowcap, or continue on the ridge developing above pt. 3334m. to the summit ($3\frac{1}{2}$ h. from hut).

<u>North-East (Follats) Ridge</u>. The most attractive climb on the mtn. from the Panossière hut. PD. Descended by F. Grob, R. Helbling, E. Labhardt, August, 1896.

208

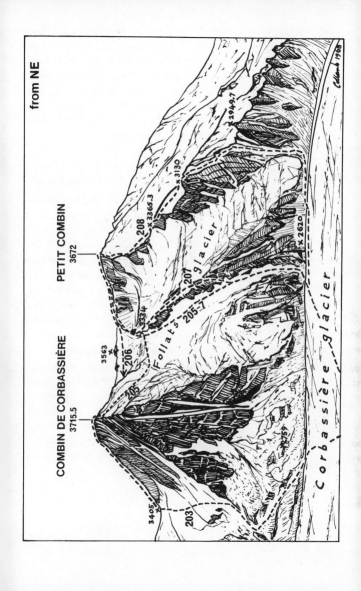

from NE

COMBIN DE CORBASSIÈRE
3715.5

PETIT COMBIN
3672

2949.7

x 3130

208
x 3365.3

207

Follats 205.7

glacier

x 2610

3334

x 3563

206

205

3405

203?

x 759

Corbassière glacier

Collund 1968

208 From the Panossière hut slant NW across the Corbassière gl. to reach the W side at 2500m. Above in the ridge flank, a long couloir comes down between pts. 2949.7m. and 3130m. Climb this couloir to the ridge and follow the loose easy crest over pt. 3130m. into a slight depression below a triangular snow slope. Go up this direct and over pt. 3365.3m. to a short descent on shale from where a fine snow crest rises progressively to the summit (5 h. from hut).

North-West Ridge. A very good mixed climb, rarely done. PD+. First ascent: J. Guigoz, E. Stettler, 5 August, 1936.

209 From the Brunet hut a good path winds S to the Sery chalets (2233m.) and continues SW to the Pindin chalet (2384m.), then over a big stream and across a grassy bluff to a tarn (2373m.) and the Nicliri chalets (2492m.). Take a continuation track SW to cross a double stream S, then contour grassy rock slopes to moraines below N side of mtn. Cross the base of a large lateral moraine and ascend the moraine trench between the latter and the next moraine E, passing a small lake and aiming to reach the foot of the NW ridge, whose first riser is marked pt. 2932.5m. (3 h.). Ascend a steep little debris facet to the top of this initial riser, then go along a fairly narrow but easy broken rock crest, with short sections on snow, up a final rock step to a slight shoulder where a short steep snow slope leads to the upper snow ridge. Follow this in a fine position, cornice on R, up to a narrow constricted section. Crevasses from the L (E) can cut the ridge at this pt. Cross a schrund and climb the 100m. summit slope, steep and often icy, to the large snow shoulder adjoining the summit snowcap which is further E (4 h., 7 h. from Brunet hut).

By-Valsorey-Velan frontier ridge

A series of secondary summits, those to E of Col du Sonadon being notable viewpoints which are visited quite often while those to W of this pt. are rarely climbed. Mt. Velan itself stands apart in a class of its own.

MONT AVRIL 3346.9m.

LK 1346, 1366. A renowned viewpoint, accessible in a dry season without touching snow. In spring, a popular ski touring summit. First recorded ascent: C.E. & W. Mathews with A. Simmond, 20 August, 1856.

South-East Spur (from Fenêtre de Durand). A rough walk, F.

210 From the Fenêtre de Durand, Rtes. 167 and 168, follow a track over grass, scree and broken rock, sometimes with snow patches, to a large cairn on the summit (1½ h.). About 4 h. from Chanrion hut.

TÊTE BLANCHE 3418m.

211 LK 1366. Primarily a good viewpoint, reached from the Amiante hut by a small track NE over scree to a rounded rock spur which conceals the summit. Do not take a horizontal track E towards a col/gap. Instead climb a little track further L on to the rock barrier overlooking gap (cairn). Now trend R on the S slopes up scree and snow to summit, F (1¼ h.). First ascent: F.W. Jacomb with J.B. & M. Croz, 7 August, 1861.

GRANDE TÊTE DE BY 3587.8m.

LK 1366. The main summit on the frontier ridge between Mt.

Gelé and Mt. Velan, climbed with little difficulty from almost
any direction. However, rock terrible. Often visited from
the Amiante hut. First ascent: surveyors, 7 July, 1894.
First British ascent: T.H. Dickson, H.V. Reade, 26 August,
1895.

South-East Flank and South Ridge. This rocky side of the mtn.
is seen from the Amiante hut, adjoining the Col d'Amiante.
Above the col and L is a partly snowy couloir which soon forks.
The L branch joins the S ridge, the R branch the SE ridge.
Avoid the R branch. Poor rock and some stonefall danger.
F+. First ascent: A. d'Annibale, G. Gatti, B. Treves, 24
August, 1913.

212 From the Amiante hut follow Rte. 196, and above the low
rockband before the col go straight up snow to the large couloir
cutting the rock wall in the summit line. Climb this on loose
rock and snow into its open L branch, normally gravel and
loose rock, to emerge at a little shoulder on the S ridge. Turn
a short step above on the L and continue up the broken crest
to summit (2 h. from hut).

LE SONADON   3578m.

LK 1346, 1366. Sometimes Mt. Sonadon. Pt. on the frontier
ridge where the neck formed by the Col du Sonadon connects
the main watershed to the Gd. Combin group further N. Excellent viewpoint, easily reached from latter col in 20 min.

AIGUILLE D'AMIANTE   3563m.

AIGUILLE VERTE   3489m.

LK 1366. Rock peaks of no great size on the frontier ridge
after Le Sonadon and before the jagged section called the Aigs.
de Valsorey. Rarely climbed.

212

AIGUILLES DE VALSOREY

LK 1366. Picturesque section of the frontier ridge running from the Col des Luisettes (3402m.) to the Col de Valsorey (3106m.), consisting of numerous blade-thin pinnacle/tower summits, seldom visited because of the rotten schist rock. Among these are Les Luisettes (3443m.), Mt. Percé (3353m.), once with a huge tunnel/window rock now fallen down, Gd. Carré (3335m.), Le Râteau (3274m.), and the five pointed Moleires de Valsorey running to the Trois Frères (3259m.), itself with three gendarme-like pts. This last mtn. has abominable rock but is probably more frequented than all the other summits put together. It is climbed from the Savoie biv. hut in 3 h. by the lower part of the SE ridge, then by a rising traverse at c. 2900m. under the E face to the depression/gully running up to a gap between the central and E summit prongs, hence from there by the short main ridge. II. First ascent: A. G. Topham with J. Maître, P. Maurys, 24 July, 1893.

COL DE VALSOREY 3106m.

213 LK 1366. Between the Trois Frères and Mt. Cordine, the most direct pass between Bourg St. Pierre and the By cwm (Ollomont). Generally used on the Ital. side for access to Mt. Velan. PD. See Rte. 214. First tourist traverse: A. Adams-Reilly, C. E. Mathews with D. & E. Balleys, 14 July, 1866.

MONT VELAN 3731m.

LK 1365, 1366. Both ends, N and S, of the broad summit mound are now measured 3731m., whereas the N end was previously regarded as the true summit. A massive, complicated mtn. carved by notable glaciers and encircled by walls of crumbling rock. In W. M. Conway's famous summary entitled "Exhausted Districts", which mostly describes the Western Pennines and which provoked the last stage of pioneering exploration in the 1890s, this mtn. is treated brusquely as "a second rate peak but it once had a first rate reputation for the doubtless inadequate reason that it commands one of the best panoramas in all the Alps". Mt. Velan was the 4th snowy peak in the Alps to be scaled by man, after the Rochemelon in 1358, Titlis in 1739, and the Buet in 1770. Today it belongs to an essential category of classical summits for peak baggers, and is remote enough to attract only the determined among their kind, for they must also be experienced alpinists. The mtn.

has a considerable following among spring skiers.

First ascent: L. J. Murith with a hunter called Genoud, 31 August, 1779. Another hunter who started with the party gave up well below the top. According to Studer, climbed by an Englishman between 1820-26, but no details are known. Certainly by W. Mathews in 1854, about the 8th ascent.

Frontier Ridge from East (Col de Valsorey). The normal rte. from Italy, fairly long and tedious, nevertheless with fine scenery. Shattered rock but mostly snow climbing. PD. All the upper part was climbed by the St. Bernard monks about 1826.

214 From the Savoie biv. hut cross grass W with a little track to the stream bed descending from the W side of the ridge coming down from the Trois Frères. Follow stream for a short way over rough ground, then cross it L to ascend with traces of a path over a loose rubble field rising towards the Col de Valsorey. Go straight up to a fairly steep snow slope which funnels into the gully leading to the col. So climb to the top, cornice possible, thus a very steep exit (3106m.). When the gully is denuded of snow it is better to use a long strip of rotten rock on its L (W) side ($1\frac{1}{2}$ h.).

From the col make a rising traverse on snow across the Swiss side for a rope length, then go straight up friable rock, approaching the rock crest of the frontier ridge but latterly skirting it still on the R side to emerge on a debris terrace just below shoulder pt. 3221m. Cross the terrace still keeping to the R (N) side of crest, to reach in 150m. a little shoulder on the crest below the next ridge pt., Mt. Cordine (3329m.). Now climb steep rotten rock, otherwise easy, just L of crest to a rock shoulder before this minor summit. From here make a fairly steep descending traverse down the NW facet of Mt. Cordine, on rock then snow (can be icy and delicate) to go round a rock toe, hugging the Valsorey gl., to attain the nearby Col des Chamois (3259m.), bergschrund probable ($1\frac{1}{2}$ h.).

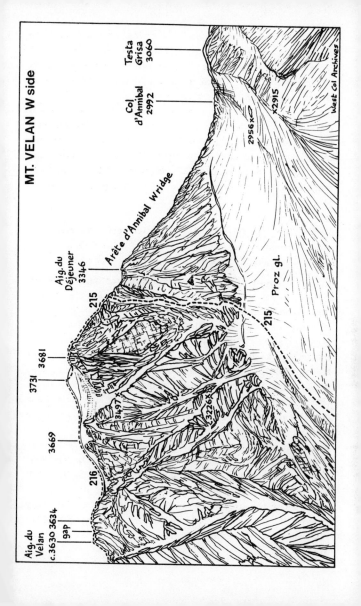

MT. VELAN W side

Testa Grisa 3060

Col d'Annibal 2992

X2915

2956 x

Aig. du Déjeuner 3346

Arête d'Annibal Wridge

215

215

Proz gl.

3681

3731

3669

3497

3326 x

216

Aig. du Velan c.3630 3634

gap

West Col Archives

Follow the frontier ridge under a rock thumb and higher up cross steep snow just below and R of the Pte. du Capucin (3396m.). On its far side traverse horizontally to the Col du Capucin (3376m.). Continue up a snowband between the gl. and the now serrated frontier ridge of the Testa d'Ariondet (3487m.) to a gl. plateau above the last icefall. Follow the L (S) side of the plateau under the Dents du Velan (3621m.) to a short snow slope leading to the last bit of rock crest where the frontier ridge has suddenly turned N ($1\frac{3}{4}$ h.). Now ascend the final rounded snow spur to the summit mound (15 min., $3\frac{1}{2}$ h. from Col de Valsorey, 5 h. from Savoie biv. hut. In descent, allow 3 h.).

<u>From West (St. Bernard Route)</u>. A long grind but easily the most frequented way up the mtn. Steep loose rock and some stonefall danger for 30 min. PD. First ascensionists.

215 From Bourg St. Bernard a little road starting at the Menouve cableway sta. goes up to a fork near the Perche stream. Keep L and follow road to the terrace at the Plan du Jeu chalets (2073m.), limited carparking (20 min.). Take a small track above in grassy slopes below the Mt. de Proz, coming to a traverse path which is followed in gradual ascent to a tributary stream (2332m.). Cross this and go up a stony grass rib on its R (S) side to moraine heaps (2795m.) under the Col de Proz. Cross these moraines to the stone-strewn N side of the Proz gl. which is followed for 15 min. until its icy surface can be trodden conveniently. Ascend near the L side, close to the W rock wall of the mtn. So reach a bergschrund in the corner below a big snow gully at the R (S) end of the wall. The first section of this gully mounts diagonally R, then bends back L for the greater part of its height up to the summit plateau (3 h.).

Get on to the broad base rock rib on immediate R of gully (stonefall), by crossing the bergschrund and keeping R of the rib crest line. Ascend this R side for 50m. above a retaining

216

wall below, then traverse diagonally L to the now better defined crest (stonefall). All the rock hereabouts is crumbling. Follow the crest on rocks and snow to where it merges into a broad staircase with snow terraces. Work up the L side of this zone until a little continuation rib on the L can be reached, about the level of a large triangular rock wall further L. (The first ascensionists appear to have passed directly under this wall, then up a shallow gully on its R side which is very exposed to stonefall). The continuation rib leads to the WSW ridge at a little rock step just above a short narrow snow crest of 25m. behind a shoulder called the Aig. du Déjeuner (3346m.). Now climb this ridge direct over a series of short steps on improving rock to the flat snowcap at the top (3681m.) ($2\frac{3}{4}$ h.). From here cross a broad snow saddle/plateau to reach the summit (15 min., $6\frac{1}{2}$ h. from Bourg St. Bernard).

North-North-West Ridge. A long and seldom followed stepped ridge of fairly sound rock with several loose sections. In good conditions, quite sure and no objective danger, recommended by those who have done it. AD with short pitches of III. First ascent: W. B. Anderson, T. Ashby, C. L. & T. G. Longstaff with J. Georges, J. Maître, P. Maurys, 18 August, 1897.

216 From the Velan hut follow the track SW for a couple of min., then leave it and move R up broken rock to the NE ridge of the Petit Velan. Follow this long easy crest of shattered rock over several little rockheads, mostly avoidable, to the N summit (3201.5m.) then S summit (3222m.) of the Petit Velan ($2\frac{1}{2}$ h.). Continue along the crest with simple scrambling down to the Col de Tseudet (3169m.) (15 min.). This col can be reached directly from below with a headslope of steep rotten rock and some stonefall hazard, in 2 h. from hut. The ridge proper commences here.

Go up the broken crest over two rockheads and several little towers, avoidable, to a snow shoulder before the step under the twin tops of the Dents de Proz (3330m.). From here it is possible to traverse across the L side of the ridge by a delicate and discontinuous snow/rock ledge system, to reach the gap on the far side of the Proz tops. Normally it is better to continue on the crest to immediately below the last sheer prow of the lower top, then traverse R under the rock wall extending below the main pinnacled top, to join the gap behind with a slight descent. Above rises the main ridge step of 200m. in light red rock, to pt. 3488m. Climb mostly on its R side, close to the crest and under several small rock pinnacles, generally loose in the lower part but steepening considerably with better rock (II) in the upper section. Parts of the crest that might be climbed have large poised blocks needing care. So reach, keeping R at the top, pt. 3488m. (2 h.).

Scramble along to the next gap and cross this, loose rock and snow, to follow up the next ridge step of 100m. This is a sharp edge of sound rock with several pleasant pitches (II, moves of III). Halfway up, a double gendarme is turned on L side into a nick, and continued with steep interesting climbing to pt. 3565m. An exposed and barely rising crest of large wedged blocks is now crossed to finish up two short steps of grey rock divided by a snow neck. The last step is turned R across a wall and up a nice chimney to exit at the sharp top of the Aig. du Velan (c. 3630m.) (1¼ h.). From here two rope lengths along the delightful horizontal and crenellated crest with good rock lead to a narrow V gap. Get into this without difficulty by descending on the L (E) side. Climb the far side up a wall L of the slightly overhanging crest with sloping holds (III) and rejoin the crest behind with a long stride. Or turn the overhang R by a rising traverse up cracks (III+). Either way, a pitch of 12m. So traverse the tower above the gap, descend to cross another gap and continue along the exposed crest with fine climbing, the highest tooth being pt. 3634m. before this pleasant section goes down a little in short steps to

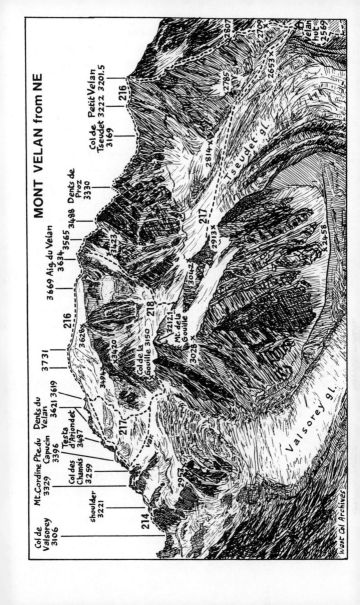

MONT VELAN from NE

Col de Valsorey 3106
shoulder 3221
214
Mt. Cordine 3329
Pte. du Velan 3396
Capucin 3621
Dents du Velan 3619
2953
Col des Chamois 3259
Testa d'Ariondet 3497
217
Var.
3404
x3420
3629
3731
Col de la Gouille 3150
218
3669 Aig. du Velan
3634
3565
3488
Dents de Proz 3330
216
3212.1
Mt. de la Gouille 3028 X
3014.2
216
2913 X
217
Col de Petit Velan 3222
Tseudet 3201.5
3169
216
2814 X
2785
2709 X
2653
2807
x 2758
Velan hut 2569
B
Valsorey gl.
Tseudet gl.

West Col Archives

a snow saddle where the rock ends (30 min.).

Above, take a nice snow crest, quite short, to a shoulder (3669m.) marking the N end of the Dôme du Velan plateau. Cross this SE and finally E to reach the summit (30 min., 7 h. from Velan hut).

Col de la Gouille and Valsorey Glacier. The normal rte. from the Velan hut and marginally the easiest way up the mtn. An excellent gl. expedition, the crevasses become tiresome after mid season. PD-. Climbed by this combination before 1860.

217 From the Velan hut follow the moraine track SSW to reach the Tseudet gl. near pt. 2653m. Work up stones keeping R, under rocky slopes, to within 100m. distance of the vague corner marked by pt. 2814m. Here move L (ESE) across the gl. above a wide broken crevassed section, crossing moraine banks, stones and ice with a few parallel crevasses. Go right across to below the rock wall of Mt. de la Gouille, and follow up below it on rocks and snow with a few crevasses extending towards you from rognon pt. 3097m. Work a little R into the snow basin beyond and go up the rock slope under the Col de la Gouille at the back. Climb this on debris and broken rock (track) with a chain handrail at the top, to the ridge saddle (3150m.) (2 h.).

On the other side descend a steep broken wall direct with another chain for 60m. to an area of rubble lying on a big snow ribbon alongside the lower icefall of the Valsorey gl. Follow this ribbon SW under the Gouille ridge to the gl. plateau above the icefall. Move L (S) into the middle of the gl. and climb in the middle of a slope (crevasses) between a rock island surrounded by ice cliffs on R and a more crevassed area to L. Higher up trend R away from terraced icebands (3461m.) below the Testa d'Ariondet, but when level with the top of them trend L again into a shallow gl. trench running up below the Dents du Velan. Here you join the last section of Rte. 214, which is

220

followed to the summit (3 h. , 5 h. from Velan hut).

If the crevasses above the first gl. plateau after the lower icefall are very bad, cross the plateau SE to the Col des Chamois (3259m.) in the frontier ridge, where Rte. 214 can be followed with few crevasse obstacles.

218 By North-East Facet of Aig. du Velan. The most direct way to the summit from the Velan hut. A varied and interesting mixed climb, the best of its kind on the mtn. AD. First ascent: M. & Mme. J. Bianchi, probably July, 1949. In winter (with more direct finish to the Aig.): Mlle. B. Koslowska with J. Jenny, 4 January, 1975.

From Velan hut follow Rte. 217 across Tseudet gl. and return R above or below rognon 3097m. up increasingly crevassed slopes SW, otherwise easy, to below the constricted icefall narrows under the N face complex (2 h.). Traverse R (NW) on snow to mount scree and easy rock starting at 3050m. , to a gap between two pinnacles on the lowest part of the spur coming down from pt. 3565m. on the NNW ridge. From the gap turn the upper pinnacle easily on the L, rejoin the crest and climb it pleasantly on fairly good rock to where the spur is disconnected by an ice gully falling to the R. Step on to the snow facet immediately L and climb this for 250m. direct in a fine position at c. 48° near the top. Below the NNW ridge, enter a snow gully from the R and go up its bed to the snow nick between the two uppermost steps on the NNW ridge immediately below the Aig. du Velan summit ($2\frac{1}{2}$ h.). Then as for Rte. 216 to summit of Mt. Velan ($1\frac{1}{4}$ h. , $5\frac{3}{4}$ h. from hut).

Addenda

PENNINE ALPS EAST

page

17   3 lines from bottom, for sh. 282 read 283.

24   Saas Grund and Weissmies hut. Triftalp cableway has been inoperative in the late 1970s.

29   As for p. 24.

44   Fletschhorn N face. Unconfirmed winter ascent by H. G. & K. Müller, end December, 1971. Certainly by A. & L. Montani, A. Palecari, 4 January, 1975.

59   Weissmies N ridge in winter: R. Schmid, F. Schnarf, 5-6 January, 1964.

96   Dom hut now enlarged with 75 places. New Mischabel hut built at 3332m. in 1976.

97   Bordier hut destroyed by fire in 1977, being rebuilt for 1980.

123   Alphubel W ridge of N summit, in winter: F. Bircher, H. Müller, 23 February, 1964.

138   Leiterspitzen traverse in winter: L. Imesch, G. Willisch, 10 January, 1976.

140   Dom first winter ascent. Spencer party was preceded by J. Krönig and party, 3 March, 1891.

PENNINE ALPS CENTRAL

20   3 lines from bottom, for sh. 282 read 283.

32   Arben bivouac hut c. 3200m. now open below S face of Obergabelhorn. Turtmann hut enlarged 1977.

36   Weisshorn hut enlarged 1976.

43   Col de la Dent Blanche bivouac hut 3540m. opened 1976 with 15 places.

69   Rothorngrat in winter: R. Arnold, M. Scherbaum, 10 January, 1976.

92   Obergabelhorn N face descended on ski: M. Butscher, K. Jeschke, 16 July, 1977.

104   Viereselsgrat in winter: M. Siegenthaler, R. Willy, 22 -23 February, 1975.

109   Dent Blanche NNW ridge, guideless British ascent (9th): G. C. Band, J. Streetly, 19 July, 1952. Solo in winter: A. Georges, 19-20 March, 1976.

113   Dent Blanche NNE face original rte., British ascent: J. Barry, D. Nicholls, 1976 (12 h.).

116   Col de la Dent Blanche. See p. 43 above.

136   Margherita hut to be rebuilt in 1979 with places for 120. This hut site not usable again until 1980.

151   Rte. 116, line 3, for c. 1850m. read c. 1950m.

152   Line 8, for W side read E side.

166   Santa Caterina ridge first British guideless ascent: G. C. Band, R. R. E. Chorley, 28 June, 1952.

168   Via Brioschi. First British ascent party was much earlier than stated. O. K. Williamson with J. Maître, H. Fuchs, 1911.

172   Dufourspitze first winter ascent. The guide B. Aymond was also in the party.

206   Liskamm Neruda Rte. Welzenbach couloir slope variation descended on ski by M. Butscher, K. Jeschke, 9 July, 1977. Party measured this section as having an angle of 53°.

207   Blanchet Rte. First British ascent: C. W. F. Noyce, J. R. Sadler, 11 August, 1959.

208   Liskamm NE face direct, W summit, in winter: P. Etter, V. W. de Wallenstadt, 13-14 January, 1963.

227   Breithorn NW face. For historical muddles concerning this face see in general Welzenbach's Climbs by E. B. Roberts. Bethmann-Hollweg rte. descended on ski by M. Butscher, K. Jeschke, 10 July, 1978 (2½ h.). British ascent of Welzenbach rte. by J. Burslem, A. Morgan, D. Robbins, July, 1975. In 1977 another rte. line further R was made and designated WNW face. In regard to Addenda note on p. 355, some 15 days earlier Helmut Kiene also climbed solo a new variation start to the Trift-jigrat, on 3 August, 1973.

232   Cesare e Giorgio biv. hut is shown at foot of rockband,

but should be indicated near top of this rockband and is approached by traversing at a level slightly higher than rockband itself.

235 NE Spur Gendarme 4106, in winter: U. Manera, C. Santunione, 3 March, 1975.

242 Matterhorn, last line of preamble, for Gervasatti read Gervasutti.

256 Matterhorn N face. P, and not 'T', Carruthers. First winter solo ascent: T. Hasegawa, 14-16 February, 1977. Repeated by W. Merhar, 8 March, 1977 in $6\frac{1}{2}$ h.

258 Matterhorn W face in winter: R. Albertini, M. Barmasse, I. Menabreaz, L. Pession, A. Tamone, A. & O. Squinobal, 11-12 January, 1978.

258 Matterhorn E face in winter: R. Arnold, G. Bumann, C. Pralong, 27-28 February, 1975.

300 Praderio biv. hut. R. N. Campbell complains he found no stove in 1976. We emphasise frequently that parties visiting unwardened biv. huts must take their own stoves, even if a particular hut was originally furnished with its own cooker, etc.

INDEX OF ROUTES SHOWN ON DIAGRAMS

Route number	Diagram on page(s)	Route number	Diagram on page(s)
3	73	40	47
4	73, 78, 83, 96	41	47
5	70, 73, 83	42	55
6	96	43	47
7	96, 141	44	47
8	104	45	47, 58
9	129	48	64, 67
15	138	49	64, 67
16	126	50	64
19	73	51	64, 67
20	35, 159	52	64, 67
21	37, 40	53	64, 67
22	47	54	64, 67, 73
23	37, 40	55	73
24	37	56	35, 70, 73
25	37, 40	57	73
26	37, 40	58	73
27	40	59	73
28	42, 47	60	78, 83
29	42	61	35, 78, 83
30	37, 40, 42	62	83
31	47	63	83
32	47	64	78
33	47	65	78, 83
34	47	66	78, 83
35	47	67	83
36	47	68	83
37	47	69	78, 88
38	47	70	78, 83
39	47	71	83

Route number	Diagram on page(s)	Route number	Diagram on page(s)
72	83	104	117
73	88	105	117
74	88	106	117
75	88	107	117
76	88	108	111, 126
77	35, 78, 83, 152	109	122, 126
78	93	110	122, 126
79	93	111	126
80	93	112	122
81	93	113	126
82	96	114	126
83	96	115	129
84	96	116	129
85	96	121	134
86	104	122	134
87	104	123	134
88	104	124	134, 138
89	104	125	134, 138
90	104, 107	127	141
91	104, 107	128	141
92	107	132	141, 157
93	107	133	157
94	107	134	157
95	104, 107	136	35
96	104	137	35, 141, 156
97	117, 122	138	157
98	122	139	152
99	129	140	152, 157
100	122, 126	141	157
101	111, 117, 126	142	156, 157
102	111, 117, 122	143	152, 159
103	117	144	157

226

Route number	Diagram on page(s)	Route number	Diagram on page(s)
145	157	192	195, 204
146	152	193	195, 201, 204
147	152	194	198
148	141	195	201, 204
149	141	196	198
150	152	197	201, 204
152	141, 152	198	201, 204
153	141, 152, 163	199	204
154	141, 152, 163	203	209
155	152	205	209
156	152	206	209
157	152, 167	207	209
159	152	208	209
160	152, 167	210	198
163	152, 167	212	198
164	152	213	219
168	126	214	219
181	201	215	215
182	219	216	215, 219
188	195	217	219
189	195, 204	218	219

General Index

Aigs. Rouges d'Arolla 99
- hut 27
Aiguillette biv. hut 140
Amiante, Aig. d' 212
- Col d' 196
- hut 186
Aosta hut 31
Aouille Tseuque 164
- Col de l' 164
Arête, Pte. de la Gde. 33
Ariondet, Testa d' 216
Aroletta chain 170
Arolla, Pigne d' 94
Arolla village 16
Avril, Mt. 211
Ayace, Col d' 170

Balme, Mt. de la 171
Barnes, Pte. 68
Berlon, Col 169
Bertol, Col de 23,61
- Dts. de 61
- hut 22
- Pte. de 59
Bionaz 19
Blanche de Perroc 41
Blanche, Tête 211
Blanchen, Col E de 149,158
- Col W de 160
- Grand 145,148
- Petit 158
Bocheresse, Col de 189

Boette, Pte. de 160
Bouquetins 61
- biv. hut 23
- Central 63
- Col des 32,69
- Col des Dts. des 63
- South Peak 66
Bourg St. Bernard 18,186
Bourg St. Pierre 18
Boussine, Tour de 193
Boveire, Aigs. de 206
- Col de 205
- Combin de 205
Brenay, Col du 95
Brulé, Col du Mt. 33,71
- Mt. 71
Brunet hut 184

Capucin, Col du 216
Cervo, Mte. 166
Châble, Le 17
Chamois, Col des 214
Chanrion hut 30
Chardoney, Bec du 168
- Col du 169,170
Chaux, Col de la 135
Cheilon, Col de 112,125
- Mt. Blanc de 110
Chermotane, Col de 24,26,94
Chèvres, Pas de 28,98
- Pte. du Pas de 98
Clapier, Mt. 181

Collon, Col 25, 74
- Col du Petit Mt. 91
- hut, Col 33
- Mt. 81
- Petit Mt. 91
Combin, Grand 191
- Petit 208
Corbassière, Combin de 206
Cordine, Mt. 214
Cornet, Colle 144
Crêt, Col du 29, 133
Crête du Plan, Pte. de la 61
Crête Sèche, Col de 169, 170, 172
Crevaye, Becca 176
Croissant, Aig. du 194
- Col du 194

Darbonneire, Cols de 109
- Pte. de 109
Division, Col de la 32
Dix barrage 17
- hut 27
Douves Blanches N 54
Douves Blanches S 56

Echos de Collon 80
Epicoune(e), Bec d' 165
- Col d' 165
- Gd. 164
Evêque, Col de l' 24, 75
- L' 75
- Mitre de l' 79

Faudery, Becca di 176
- Col de 170
- Trident de 177

Fenêtre de Durand 173
Fionnay 18
Fiorio, Pta. 181
Fort, Col du Petit Mt. 136
- hut, Mt. 30
- Mt. 136

Gelé, Col du Mt. 172
- cableway, Mt. 18, 30
- Mt. 171
Genevois, Pte. des 48
Gentianes, Col des 136
Glacier hamlet 20
Gouille, Col de la 220
Grand Combin 191
Grand Tavé 189
Grand Tête de By 211
Grafeneire, Combin de 193

Labié, Becque 161, 162
Lacs, Becca des 158
Lia, Becca de la 190
Lire Rose, Col de 112
Luette, La 127

Maisons Blanches, Col des 205
- Les 205
Mauvoisin 18
Meitin, Col du 202
- Combin du 205
Mitre, Col de la 79, 81
Mitre de l'Evêque 79
Moleires de Valsorey 213
Momin, Col de 135

Morion Central 179
- N 179
- S 180
Mt. Fort hut 30

Ollomont 19
Oren, Col d' 145,147
- Ptes. d' 91
Otanes, Col des 189
Otemma, Col d' 161,162
- Pte. d' 124

Panossière, Col de 206
- hut 184
Pantalons Blancs biv. hut 28
Parrain, Le 132
Perroc, Blanche de 41
- Dt. de 44
Picion, Becca 165
Pigne d'Arolla 94
Place Moulin 19
Plateau du Couloir 199
Pleureur, Le 128
Prafleuri hut 28
Prarayer 31
Proz, Dts. de 218

Rayette, Becca 165
- Col de la Rayette 168
Regondi biv. hut 143
Riedmatten, Col de 98
Rochers du Bouc 29
Rosablanche, La 132
Rosses, Bec de (photo) 138
Rouge, Col du Mt. 112
Rouges d'Arolla, Aigs. 99

Rouges hut, Aigs. 27
Ruinette, La 121

St. Bernard pass 18,186
St. Laurent hut 29
Sale, La 130
Sassa biv. hut 140
Sasse, Bec de la 160
Savoie biv. hut 187
Serpentine, Col de la 110,113
- La 110
Severeu, Col de 133
Singla, La 145,150
Sonadon, Col du 197
- Le 212
Spataro biv. hut 142
Super St. Bernard 18,186

Tavé des Chasseurs 189
Tavé, Gd. 189
Tête Blanche 211
Tête de By, Gd. 211
Tortin 17
Tournelon Blanc 190
- Col du 190
Trident de Faudery 177
Trois Frères, Les 213
Tsa, Aig. de la 52
- Col de la 59
- hut 22
Tsa de Tsan, Col de 71,72
Tsalion, Dt. de 50
- Pte. de 49
Tsarmine, Col de 38,39
Tsena Réfien, Col de 98

Tsessette, Combin de 192
Tseudet, Col de 217
Tsijiore Nouve, Col de 98

Valpelline 19
Valsorey, Aigs. de 213
- Col de 213, 214

- Combin de 200
- hut 185
Vasevay, Col du 130

Veisivi, Gde. Dt. de 39
- Petite Dt. de 36
Velan, Aig. du 218, 221
- Dts. du 216
- hut 186
- Mt. 213
- Petit 217
Verte, Aig. 212
Vignettes hut 25, 26
Vouasson, Pte. de 109